SMART GUIDE

CREATIVE HOMEOWNER®

stairs & railings

step-by-step projects

CREATIVE HOMEOWNER®, Upper Saddle River, New Jersey

COPYRIGHT © 1997, 1999, 2008

CRE🏠TIVE
HOMEOWNER®

A Division of Federal Marketing Corp.
Upper Saddle River, NJ

SMARTGUIDE®and Creative Homeowner® are registered trademarks of Federal Marketing Corp.

Author: Jeff Beneke
Editor: Fran J. Donegan
Photo Researcher: Robyn Poplasky
Junior Editor: Jennifer Calvert
Editorial Assistant: Nora Grace
Digital Imaging Specialist: Frank Dyer
Graphic Designers: Maureen Mulligan, Michael James Allegra
Illustrators: Clarke Barre, James Randolph (except where noted)
Cover Photography: Brian Vanden Brink, architect: John Gillespie
Smart Guide® Series Cover Design: Clarke Barre

Creative Homeowner
Vice President and Publisher: Timothy O. Bakke
Production Director: Kimberly H. Vivas
Art Director: David Geer
Managing Editor: Fran J. Donegan

Current Printing (last digit)
10 9 8 7 6 5 4 3 2

Manufactured in the United States of America

Smart Guide: Stairs & Railings
First published as *Quick Guide: Stairs & Railings*
Library of Congress Control Number: 2007933888
ISBN-10: 1-58011-393-1
ISBN-13: 978-1-58011-393-9

CREATIVE HOMEOWNER®
www.creativehomeowner.com

Metric Conversion

Length

1 inch	25.4 mm
1 foot	0.3048 m
1 yard	0.9144 m
1 mile	1.61 km

Area

1 square inch	645 mm²
1 square foot	0.0929 m²
1 square yard	0.8361 m²
1 acre	4046.86 m²
1 square mile	2.59 km²

Volume

1 cubic inch	16.3870 cm³
1 cubic foot	0.03 m³
1 cubic yard	0.77 m³

Common Lumber Equivalents

Sizes: Metric cross sections are so close to their U.S. sizes, as noted below, that for most purposes they may be considered equivalents.

Dimensional lumber	1 x 2	19 x 38 mm
	1 x 4	19 x 89 mm
	2 x 2	38 x 38 mm
	2 x 4	38 x 89 mm
	2 x 6	38 x 140 mm
	2 x 8	38 x 184 mm
	2 x 10	38 x 235 mm
	2 x 12	38 x 286 mm
Sheet sizes	4 x 8 ft.	1200 x 2400 mm
	4 x 10 ft.	1200 x 3000 mm
Sheet thicknesses	¼ in.	6 mm
	⅜ in.	9 mm
	½ in.	12 mm
	¾ in.	19 mm
Stud/joist spacing	16 in. o.c.	400 mm o.c.
	24 in. o.c.	600 mm o.c.

Capacity

1 fluid ounce	29.57 mL
1 pint	473.18 mL
1 quart	1.14 L
1 gallon	3.79 L

Temperature

Celsius = Fahrenheit – 32 x ⅝
Fahrenheit = Celsius x 1.8 + 32

Photo Credits

page 1: davidduncanlivingston.com **page 3:** *top* Jessie Walker; *center* Jessie Walker, architect: Gary Frank; *bottom* davidduncanlivingston.com **page 5:** *right* Jessie Walker, design: Jane Levy Designs; *bottom* left Phillip H. Ennis Photography; *top left* Jessie Walker **page 17:** *top right* Jessie Walker; *bottom right* Gary David Gold/CH; *bottom left* Tony Giammarino/Giammarino & Dworkin, architect: William Prillaman; *top left* Jessie Walker **page 27:** *top right* courtesy of Wolman Lumber; *bottom* Randall Perry; *top left* Walter Chandoha **page 33:** *top right* Brian Vanden Brink, architect: John Gillespie; *bottom right* Jessie Walker, architect: David Frankel; *bottom left* Jessie Walker, architect: Jim Tharp; *top left* davidduncanlivingston.com **page 43:** *top right & bottom right* Jessie Walker; *left* davidduncanlivingston.com **page 47:** *top right & bottom right* Jessie Walker; *bottom left* courtesy of Calvert USA, Inc.; *top left* Jessie Walker, architect: Gary Frank **page 53:** *right & top* Jessie Walker; *bottom left* davidduncanlivingston.com **page 69:** *all* Jessie Walker **page 79:** *top right* Jerry Pavia; *bottom*

right John Parsekian/CH; *bottom left* Karen Bussolini; *top left* carolynbates.com, design & installation: Paul Wieczoreck, Champlain Valley Landscaping **page 80:** *illustration* Robert LaPointe **pages 81–85:** *all* John Parsekian/CH **page 86:** *illustration* Elayne Sears, Michele Angle Ferrar, Robert LaPointe **page 87:** *top right* carolynbates.com, design & installation: Land-shapes; *bottom right* Jerry Pavia; *bottom left* Michael S. Thompson; *top left* Karen Bussolini **page 88:** *top* Karen Bussolini; *bottom* carolynbates.com, design & installation: Paul Wieczoreck, Champlain Valley Landscaping **page 89:** *top* Gay Bumgarner; *bottom* Lee Anne White **page 90:** *top* Alan & Linda Detrick; *bottom* Charles Mann **page 91:** *both* Charles Mann **pages 92–93:** *illustrations* Elayne Sears, Michele Angle Ferrar, Robert LaPointe; *bottom right* Jerry Pavia; *bottom left* Charles Mann; *top left* carolynbates.com, design & installation: Michael Lawrence Associates, Distinctive Landscaping **page 94:** *left & top right* Alan & Linda Detrick; *bottom right* Jerry Howard

contents

safety first

Though all the designs and methods in this book have been reviewed for safety, it is not possible to overstate the importance of using the safest construction methods possible. What follows are reminders; some do's and don'ts of basic carpentry. They are not substitutes for your own common sense.

- *Always* use caution, care, and good judgment when following the procedures described in this book.

- *Always* be sure that the electrical setup is safe; be sure that no circuit is overloaded and that all power tools and electrical outlets are properly grounded. Do not use power tools in wet locations.

- *Always* read container labels on paints, solvents, and other products; provide ventilation, and observe all other warnings.

- *Always* read the manufacturer's instructions for using a tool, especially the warnings.

- *Always* use hold-downs and push sticks whenever possible when working on a table saw. Avoid working short pieces if you can.

- *Always* remove the key from any drill chuck (portable or press) before starting the drill.

- *Always* pay deliberate attention to how a tool works so that you can avoid being injured.

- *Always* know the limitations of your tools. Do not try to force them to do what they were not designed to do.

- *Always* make sure that any adjustment is locked before proceeding. For example, always check the rip fence on a table saw or the bevel adjustment on a portable saw before starting to work.

- *Always* clamp small pieces firmly to a bench or other work surface when using a power tool on them.

- *Always* wear the appropriate rubber or work gloves when handling chemicals, moving or stacking lumber, or doing heavy construction.

- *Always* wear a disposable face mask when you create dust by sawing or sanding. Use a special filtering respirator when working with toxic substances and solvents.

- *Always* wear eye protection, especially when using power tools or striking metal on metal or concrete; a chip can fly off, for example, when chiseling concrete.

- *Always* be aware that there is seldom enough time for your body's reflexes to save you from injury from a power tool in a dangerous situation; everything happens too fast. Be *alert!*

- *Always* keep your hands away from the business ends of blades, cutters, and bits.

- *Always* hold a circular saw firmly, usually with both hands so that you know where they are.

- *Always* use a drill with an auxiliary handle to control the torque when large-size bits are used.

- *Always* check your local building codes when planning new construction. The codes are intended to protect public safety and should be observed to the letter.

- *Never* work with power tools when you are tired or under the influence of alcohol or drugs.

- *Never* cut tiny pieces of wood or pipe using a power saw. Cut small pieces off larger pieces.

- *Never* change a saw blade or a drill or router bit unless the power cord is unplugged. Do not depend on the switch being off; you might accidentally hit it.

- *Never* work in insufficient lighting.

- *Never* work while wearing loose clothing, hanging hair, open cuffs, or jewelry.

- *Never* work with dull tools. Have them sharpened, or learn how to sharpen them yourself.

- *Never* use a power tool on a workpiece—large or small—that is not firmly supported.

- *Never* saw a workpiece that spans a large distance between horses without close support on each side of the cut; the piece can bend, closing on and jamming the blade, causing saw kickback.

- *Never* support a workpiece from underneath with your leg or other part of your body when sawing.

- *Never* carry sharp or pointed tools, such as utility knives, awls, or chisels, in your pocket. If you want to carry such tools, use a special-purpose tool belt with leather pockets and holders.

chapter 1

basic design

Defining the Stairway

Traditionally, stairbuilding was left to the most experienced member of the carpentry crew, or even subcontracted to a specialist. There were several reasons for this. First, staircase construction defies standardization. Each stairway is different, if only by a matter of inches or even fractions of inches. Unlike most carpentry tasks, in stairbuilding a slight variation in dimensions can throw the whole project off. Second, good-quality staircase construction used to demand fine joinery techniques, such as the use of dovetails to join balusters with treads. Third, stairbuilding demands mathematical skills combined with accurate measurements. Finally, stairbuilding has a vocabulary and order of tasks all its own.

Today, stair construction doesn't cry for complex joinery to ensure a long life. And mastering the other skills is no more difficult than following the step-by-step approach to stairbuilding outlined in this book. The first step is to familiarize yourself with the vocabulary used by stairbuilders.

Staircase Shapes

Stairs vary in shapes and sizes. In some circumstances, your choices may be limited by space or budget; in others, you are free to build exactly according to your wishes.

Straight-Run Stairs. The most common, most basic, and simplest staircase to build is a straight-run. As the name implies, this is a stairway that rises in a straight line from bottom to top. The ease of construction of straight-run stairs lies in the fact that the stringers, treads, and risers (if used) are identical.

Straight-run stairs are long, however, and sometimes difficult to fit into a floor plan. Often, they are built against a wall. Where space is not a problem, such as to a basement, straight stairs should be your first choice.

L-Shaped Stairs. An L-shaped staircase consists of two short straight-runs set at right angles to each other and separated by a landing. An L-shaped stairway isn't as long in one direction as straight-run stairs, although it does require as much or more total floor space. It is most often built into a corner, with a wall running along one side. The L-shaped staircase is versatile in that the landing can be located at, above, or below the midpoint, which can satisfy a range of space limitations.

Winders. A winder is really a variation on an L-shaped stairway. It makes the same 90-degree turn, but it features three (sometimes four) triangular-shaped treads. Older winder designs, with the treads coming to a point, had the benefit of taking up less space than straight or L-shaped stairs. But today's codes have restricted, or even eliminated, this design. The tapered treads are considered dangerous because a person can't safely step on the narrow end.

You may be able to build a traditional winder if you're remodeling or if you're building utility stairs. Be sure to check with building officials before starting.

Straight-Run Stairs. This common staircase is the easiest to build but requires a long, straight stretch of space.

L-Shaped Stairs. This is a useful stairway to build into a corner. The landing can be located in the middle or near the top or bottom.

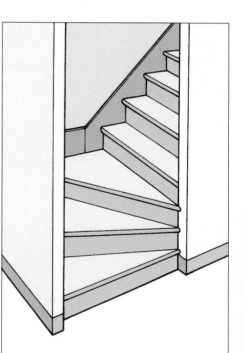

Winders. Winders function like L-shaped stairs by creating a 90-degree turn, but they can take up less floor space.

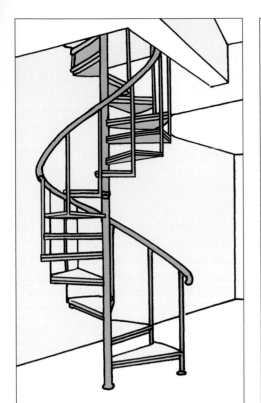

Spiral Stairs. The most compact design, spiral stairs are available as prefabricated units.

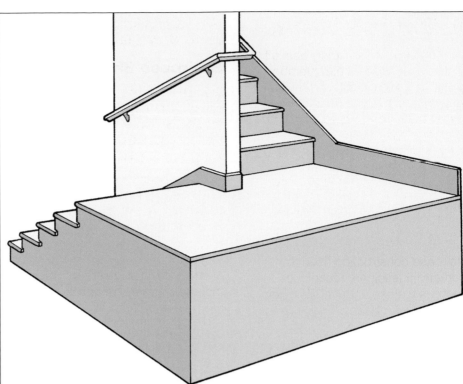

U-Shaped Stairs. This style makes a complete 180-degree turn. They are built much like L-shaped stairs but with a larger landing.

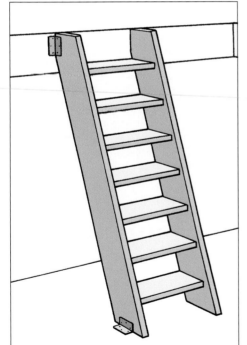

Ladders. When stairs are steeper than allowed by code, they officially become ladders. While not suitable for frequent use, a ladder can be useful for storage areas or sleeping lofts.

Spiral Stairs. Spiral stairs take up the least floor space of any stairway style. However, spiral stairs usually are not recommended for a main stairway. They compromise safety and do not allow large objects, such as furniture, to be moved up and down. Nearly all spiral stairs are built from prefabricated parts.

U-Shaped Stairs. U-shaped, or switchback, stairs are similar to L-shaped stairs except that they make a full 180-degree turn. This is accomplished usually by making the landing much larger. U-shaped stairs are fairly compact in their use of floor space and are especially favored in multistory commercial buildings.

Ladders. Technically, a stairway becomes a ladder when its slope exceeds the rise and run requirements used by codes to define a staircase. A ladder would not be suitable for regular use, but it can be an ideal utility stairway to an attic, sleeping loft, or other infrequently used space. The ladder is simple to build and takes up very little space.

Staircase Construction Styles

All of the stairs that are covered in depth in this book are "freestanding"; that is, they are capable of spanning from one level to the other without intermediate support. The stringers on these stairs provide the structural strength. Although they use the same structural framework, stairs can be divided into three general categories: closed, semi-closed, or open.

Closed vs. Open. A closed staircase has walls on both sides. If it has no walls, it is an open staircase. The most common style, the semi-closed stairway, has a wall on one side and is open on the other. The principal difference in construction of the three styles is the railing system: An open staircase requires a balustrade on both sides, semi-closed stairs require a single balustrade, and a closed stairway needs only a wall rail.

Closed vs. Open. Stairs can be enclosed by walls on one or both sides, or they can be open. Despite the visual differences, each type of stairway meets identical minimum standards.

Interior vs. Exterior. Regardless of where they are located, stairs exist to allow movement from one level to another. Nevertheless, there are some important differences in exterior and interior stairs. The most obvious difference is exposure to weather. Exterior stairs must be able to withstand all of the climate swings that your location can throw at them. Consequently, exterior stairs should be constructed of weather-resistant wood and treated with wood preservative regularly to maintain their durability.

Interior stairs must often be built within tight spaces. You may be faced with adjusting the style of staircase as well as the rise and run to keep the stairs within bounds. Exterior stairs frequently do not face such limitations and can be designed in the style and dimensions you deem best.

Exterior stairs generally are less steep than interior stairs. This more gradual slope, which is made possible by increasing the run (to between 12 and 16 inches) and decreasing the rise (to about 6 inches), is especially recommended in climates where snow and ice buildup are likely.

Exterior stairs are often quite short, and if they're also narrow—you can build them using only two stringers, which can make the use of cleats or stair brackets more appealing. By not having to cut out stringers, your job will go much faster.

Exterior stairs, especially those leading to a deck surface, are often built without risers (called open-riser stairs). This construction method is quicker and cheaper, and it minimizes wood-to-wood connections that trap dirt and moisture and therefore speed deterioration. Porch stairs can also be built with open risers, although many traditional styles enclose the riser.

The main stairway in the house, usually connecting the first and second floors, must be built strictly according to building codes. Interior stairs that are not normally visible from the main living areas of the house are sometimes referred to as utility stairs, and building codes aren't as strict when it comes to constructing these stairs. The most common type of utility stairway connects the first floor with the basement. These stairs can be built with open risers and common structural lumber. Stairs connecting the first floor with

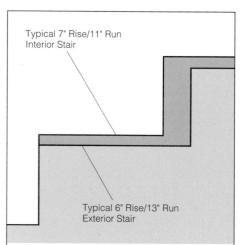

Typical 7" Rise/11" Run
Interior Stair

Typical 6" Rise/13" Run
Exterior Stair

Interior vs. Exterior. Because they're not affected by the weather, and consequently won't get icy or wet, interior stairs can be steeper than exterior stairs. Exterior stairs must be built to withstand severe weather.

the second floor, however, are a more visible part of the house's interior and are usually built with closed risers.

Your local code may specify some differences in design and materials depending on where the stairs are being built. But the principles that determine safe stairs and handrails remain the same, inside or out.

Staircase and Railing Anatomy

Like many aspects of construction, the terminology of stairbuilding differs from region to region and generation to generation. For an earlier generation, differentiating between "carriages" and "stringers," for example, was important because they were two different pieces performing two different functions. With contemporary construction methods, the differences have diminished considerably, and the two terms are often used interchangeably by stairbuilders.

Stringers

In this book, a stringer will be defined as the structural member to which the treads are attached. There are several styles of stringers, but they all function to carry the load of the stairs.

Notched Stringers. The most common style of staircase today is the notched stringer, also called a cutout stringer. Notched stringers are usually built with two-by framing lumber that is cut out in a sawtooth pattern to support treads and risers. On basement or other utility stairs, notched stringers are usually left exposed, while on other stairs they may be covered with a trim piece (sometimes called a finish stringer). Most of the stairs in this book will be built with notched stringers.

Cleated Stringers. Cleated stringers consist of unnotched stringers with wood cleats screwed to the insides to carry the treads. Bracketed stringers differ only in that the cleats are replaced by metal stair brackets, also called stair angles. Both of these styles are easy to build, but they're not particularly attractive. Thus, the cleated style is suited more to short and narrow utility stairs and porch or deck stairs mainly because they are not a large and visible architectural feature.

Mortised Stringers. Mortised stringers are similar to cleated and bracketed stringers in overall appearance, but they are tougher to build. The difference is that the treads rest within channels, or dadoes, cut on the inside faces of the stringers. A mortised stringer is likely to appeal to those seeking a custom look in open-riser stairs.

Perhaps the most apparent feature of high-quality traditional stairs is the housed stringer. This piece of high-quality wood doubles as both a stringer and skirtboard because it has mortises for treads and risers routed directly into its face. Usually, a housed stringer is attached to the

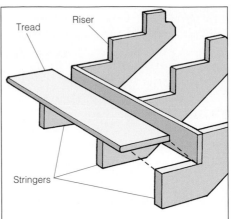

Notched Stringers. Notched stringers, usually 2x12s, are cut in a sawtooth pattern, and the cutout sections support treads and risers.

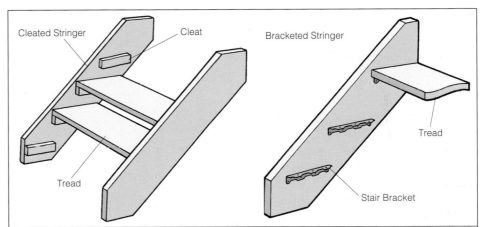

Cleated Stringers. Cleated stringers have no notches; instead, the treads are fastened to wood cleats or metal brackets.

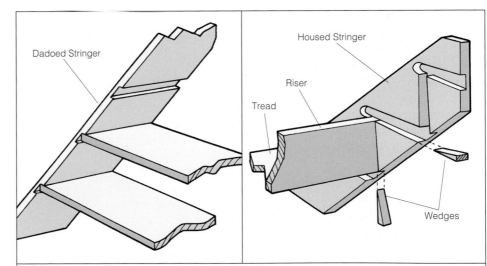

Mortised Stringers. Mortised stringers look like cleated stringers and come in two varieties: a dadoed stringer, with channels cut on the inside faces to hold the treads, and a housed stringer, which is grooved to hold treads and risers that get wedged in place.

wall framing. Treads and risers slip into the mortises and are tightened in place with wedges. The joints between treads and risers are tight and attractive. But the labor involved is excessive, requiring that the builder have special jigs and good skill in handling a router. Most housed stringers installed today are prefabricated.

Treads, Risers, and Nosings. The parts of the stairs that you can readily see consist of the treads, risers, and nosings. The tread is the horizontal part of the stair, the part that you step on when going up and down.

The riser is the vertical part of the stair, located between treads. When risers are used in the construction, the result is a "closed-riser staircase."

When risers are not used and the vertical space is left open, the staircase is called an "open riser."

The nosing is that part of the tread that overhangs the face of the riser. It is often rounded.

The Skirtboard. The term "skirtboard," as used in this book, refers to what is essentially a piece of

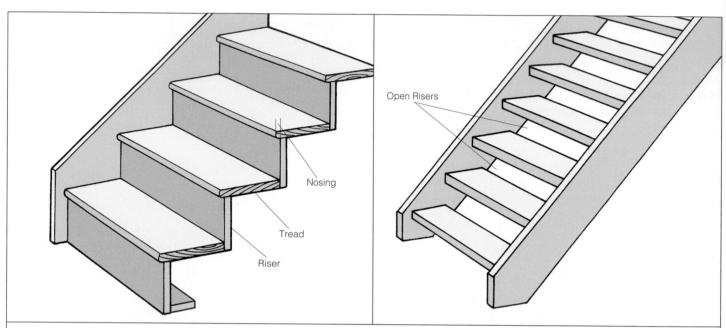

Treads, Risers, and Nosings. Treads are the horizontal boards that you step on; risers are the vertical parts that close off the back end of the treads. Nosings are the front edges of the treads that overhang the risers. Stairs without risers are called open-riser stairs.

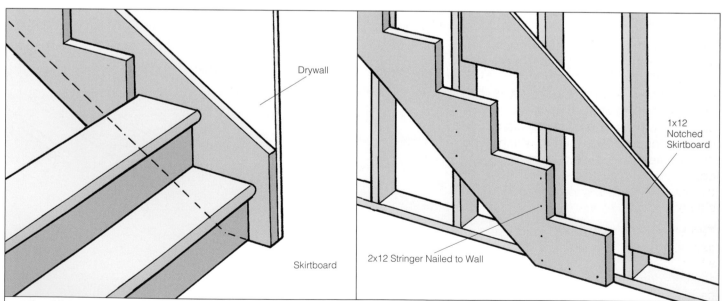

The Skirtboard. On closed or semi-closed stairs, a piece of trim called a skirtboard is installed between the stairs and a wall to protect the wall. Skirtboards may be slipped between the stringer and the wall, or they may be notched to fit over the treads and risers.

trim installed between the stairs and a wall. A skirtboard hides the structural members and protects the wall from damage. It does not perform a structural function of its own. The easiest way to install a skirtboard is to slip it behind the stringer and attach it to the wall before the treads and risers are installed. The treads and risers can then be cut for a tight fit against the skirtboard. If the stringer is going to be nailed to the wall, however, you will have to cut notches in the skirtboard for it to fit in place. The skirtboard can be laid out just like the stringers; the difference is that the cut-out sections will be reversed.

The Balustrade. The railing, or balustrade, is the entire assembly that supports the handrail. It consists of newels (or newel posts), balusters, and the handrail itself.

Newels are large vertical members to which the handrail is attached. They supply the structural support for the balustrade and are typically bolted to the house framing or the stringers.

The handrail is the part of the balustrade that the user holds on to. The handrail provides balance and support for people climbing or descending the stairs. A handrail must be sized to be graspable by users.

Balusters are small, vertical members that support the handrail. The bottom ends of balusters are usually connected to the treads on interior stairs, although the balustrades on utility stairs (as well as exterior stairs) often have upper and lower rails, to which the balusters are connected. In addition to supporting the handrail, balusters prevent falls through the side of the stairway.

The Stairwell. The stairwell is the framed shaft between floors through which the stairs pass. A typical stairwell opening has doubled two-by headers at the top and above the base of the stairs, and doubled trimmer joists running along both sides. If you are framing the stairwell, it must

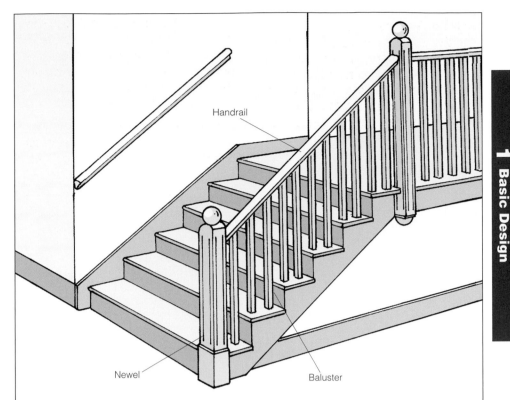

The Balustrade. Often called a railing, the balustrade includes the handrail, the balusters, or spindles, and the newels, or newel posts, at the top and bottom of the stairs.

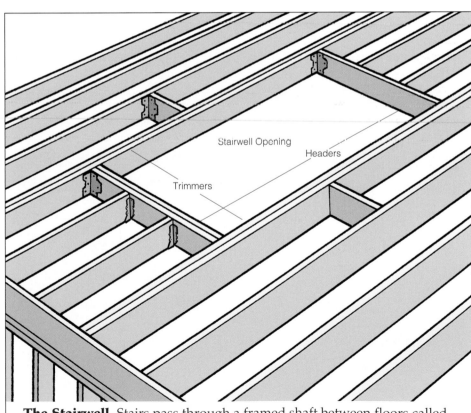

The Stairwell. Stairs pass through a framed shaft between floors called a stairwell. Headers are installed at each end of the stairwell opening, and the framing around the opening is doubled.

be wide enough to accommodate the width of the staircase plus any wall finish surfaces you plan to install. The length of the stairwell must be sufficient to allow adequate headroom. (See page 21.)

Stairway Dimensions

From the stairwell to the handrail, stairs are subject to strict building-code regulations regarding acceptable dimensions. The following is a discussion of acceptable dimensions for the parts of a staircase.

Headroom is the vertical distance measured from an imaginary line connecting the nosing on all of the treads. Most codes require a minimum of 80 inches from that line to any object above. The purpose of the headroom requirement is to prevent you from knocking your head against the ceiling or other obstruction.

If you live in a household where no one is taller than, say, 72 inches, you may feel that 80 inches of headroom is more than adequate. But stairs are not like escalators. When you use the stairs, the motion is more akin to jumping up and down than gliding smoothly. Thus, the minimal code requirement should be treated as a minimum, not a maximum. A more comfortable target for headroom is 84 inches, and even more if possible. When your space is too limited to allow for adequate headroom using conventional framing techniques, you can buy extra room with some creative framing, as shown in "Making Headroom," on page 21.

Rise is a vertical measurement, and run is horizontal. These are the most frequently referred to components of staircase design. Both are expressed in "total" and "unit" dimensions. "Total rise" is the total vertical distance that the stairs must climb. Rise is measured from finished floor surfaces.

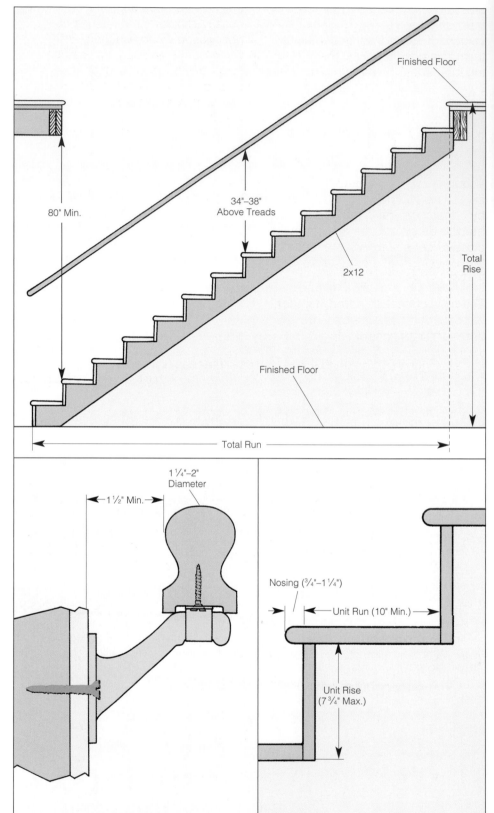

Stairway Dimensions. Building codes are specific on the requirements for staircase dimensions. The drawing gives typical requirements, but be sure to check your local code before you begin.

Most stairs are built before the finished floor surfaces have been installed, so you must compensate for these later additions. "Unit rise" is the vertical distance from one tread to the next. All of the unit rises added together should equal the total rise.

The "total run" is the amount of horizontal distance the stairway covers. "Unit run" is the horizontal distance from the face of one riser to the face of the next.

Although the nosing is part of the tread, it is addressed separately by codes. Typically, the nosing must be between ¾ and 1¼ inches on closed-riser stairs. In some jurisdictions, nosing may not be required if the treads are 11 inches or deeper.

The most critical components of good stair design are the ratio between unit rise and unit run and their consistency from one step to the next. Safety is maximized when people can use a "normal" and predictable stride up or down. Thus, codes only address unit rise and unit run. For residential stairs, codes usually stipulate that the unit rise not exceed 7¾ to 8 inches, and that the minimum unit run be 9 to 10 inches. Be sure to check your local code requirements before you start designing your stairs. Again note that these are minimums and maximums, not necessarily optimums. A stairway built to the minimum run and maximum rise is likely to feel too steep. For most people, a 7-inch rise and 11-inch run are the most comfortable.

The handrail must be located between 30 and 34 inches above the treads (some codes allow 30 to 38 inches). The handrail must be graspable, which can be ensured if it is circular and with a diameter between 1¼ inches and 2 inches. The handrail must be located at least 1½ inches from the wall.

Landings. A landing is a horizontal platform at midflight in a stair run. Landings are necessary when the stairs change directions and may be required to provide a resting area on straight stairs that rise more than 12 feet. A typical landing on an L-shaped staircase will be square, with sides as long as the stairs are wide. Codes usually address several components of width in a staircase. A common minimum width is 36 inches, measured from finished surfaces. Handrails don't affect this width. When one handrail is used, the width of the stairway at the handrail height can usually be reduced by 4 inches (to 32 inches), and if handrails are used on both sides, to 28 inches. Take into account the thickness of finish materials, such as drywall and skirtboards, when framing the stairwell opening.

The term landing also refers to the surface at the top and bottom of the stairs. It is desirable, and may be

Codes and Staircase Safety

When a staircase is properly designed and built, using it becomes second nature. Only when a staircase is poorly designed does it become a chore to use. Stairs must be built to accommodate people of all ages and physical abilities. That is why codes tend to be quite strict, and it is why you should pay close attention to them.

Staircases can be dangerous places. National statistics compiled by the Centers for Disease Control and Prevention found millions of stair-related accidents in 2003, with almost 1.8 million of them requiring hospitalization and several thousand resulting in death. The design and construction of the stairs themselves is not a major cause of these accidents, however. Poor lighting, being in a hurry, loose carpeting, and ungraspable handrails are more often the principal culprits.

Children, the elderly, and the physically disabled are the most prone to staircase accidents. This book will help you design and build safe stairs and guide you toward choosing and installing graspable handrails. But you will have to make some decisions of your own

regarding the availability of adequate lighting. Even lighting from top to bottom is recommended, and light-colored walls can be a real help. If you plan to install carpeting over your stairs, don't use deep-pile or shag carpeting. The carpeting must be installed tightly around the nosing and secured well to the rest of the stairs.

All of the stairs that are covered in depth in this book have been designed to meet or exceed typical code requirements. That doesn't ensure, however, that they will be fully satisfactory to your building inspector. Be sure to discuss your plans with the qualified authorities in your locale.

Keep in mind that code requirements are not necessarily perfect. They exist to set boundaries, minimal and maximal tolerances that cover a variety of situations and needs. When it comes to code requirements on dimensions for treads, risers, and headroom, for example, you will usually be much happier if you expand the strict standards. In the following chapters, code requirements are compared with more ideal recommendations.

required, to have a 36-inch-square landing at the top and bottom of the stairs. Also, if you have a door at the top of the stairs that swings into the stairway, you will need a landing on the stair side so that there's enough space to open the door.

Tools

You can build perfectly good stairs with relatively few tools. A basic stairbuilding tool chest consists of the following:

For Measuring and Marking: an accurate measuring tape, plumb bob, 24-inch level, framing square, and pencil.

For Cutting: a circular saw, handsaw, power drill, and plane. To increase efficiency, and perhaps accuracy as well, a power miter box, or chop saw, and a table saw or radial-arm saw will come in handy. If you want to create rounded nosings out of square-edged treads, you will need a router equipped with roundover and mortising bits. A saber saw is useful, though not essential.

For Joining: a hammer, nail set, clamps, screwdrivers (or screwdriver bits for use in your drill), chisel, and caulking gun for applying construction adhesive.

For Safety: goggles or safety glasses, dust masks, and gloves for handling pressure-treated lumber on exterior stairs.

Other Tools: The only more specialized tool that you need is a pair of inexpensive stair buttons (also called stair gauges). These buttons can be attached to a framing square to create a template that ensures accurate layouts. Dividers are another useful tool for creating a story pole to double-check the layout.

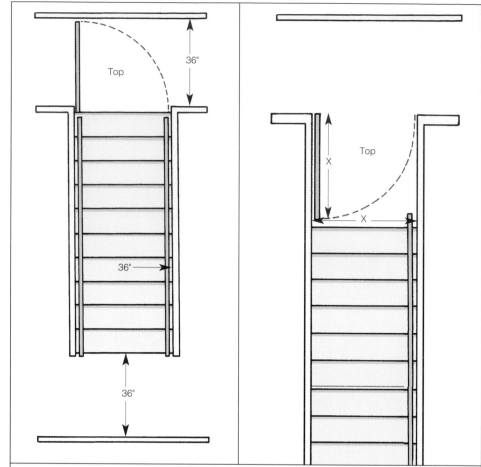

Landings. A landing is a level platform that allows the user to adjust to the new level or turn a corner. Landings are required on L-shaped stairs and should be provided at the top and bottom of all stairs. If a door swings toward a stairway, provide a landing at least as wide as the door.

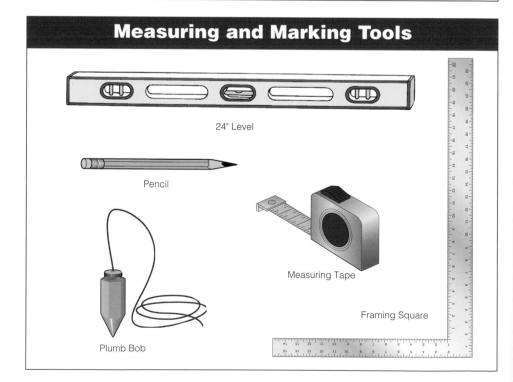

Measuring and Marking Tools

24" Level

Pencil

Plumb Bob

Measuring Tape

Framing Square

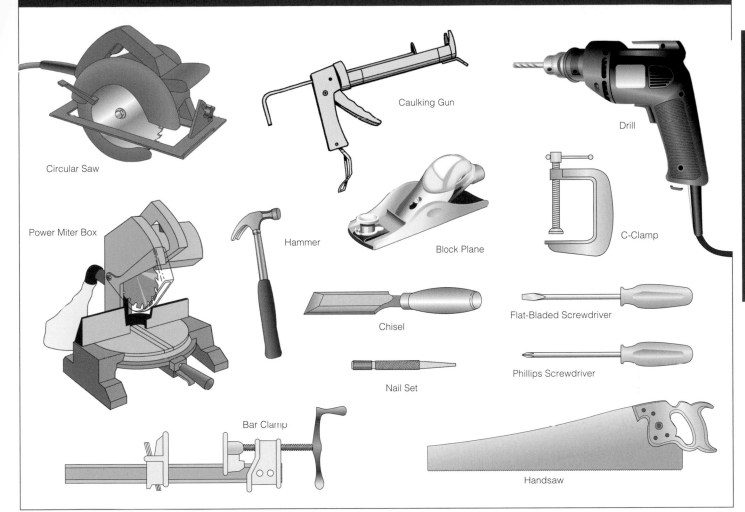

Circular Saw

Caulking Gun

Drill

Power Miter Box

Hammer

Block Plane

C-Clamp

Chisel

Flat-Bladed Screwdriver

Nail Set

Phillips Screwdriver

Bar Clamp

Handsaw

Safety and Other Specialized Tools

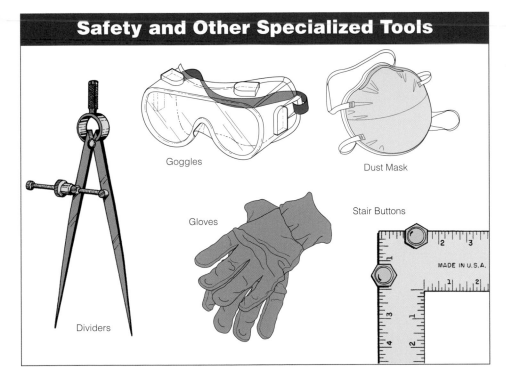

Goggles

Dust Mask

Gloves

Stair Buttons

Dividers

MADE IN U.S.A.

Materials

Most basic stair styles can be built with the lumber and other materials available at any lumberyard or building supply outlet. For common basement stairs that are meant to emphasize utility more than aesthetics, standard two-by lumber is the best choice. It is widely available in a range of widths, easy to cut and nail, and the most affordable option. Stringers are usually made from 2x10s or 2x12s, while treads can be formed with 2x4s or 2x6s.

Stringers. The stringers carry the load on your stairs, so they should be large enough and solid enough to perform their job. Pick out your stringer boards personally and carefully at the lumberyard. Look

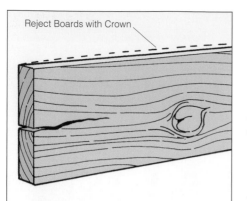

Reject Boards with Crown

Stringers. Stringers are the structural backbone of the stairs. They are usually made from 2x10s or 2x12s. Choose straight boards free of knots and splits.

for straight boards that are relatively free of knots and splits. If the ends are split, you will need to cut away the split section before laying out the stringer, so judge lengths accordingly: A 16-foot 2x12 with 12-inch-long splits on each end is effective only a 14-footer.

All of the stairs in this book are built with 2x12 stringers, but on shorter runs, such as off decks and porches, you may be able to use 2x10s. The critical difference between the two sizes is the amount of solid wood left after the notches have been cut. Codes often require that at least 3½ inches of wood remain below the cutout (see drawing), and a 2x10 frequently won't leave this much solid stock. When building exterior stairs, use pressure-treated lumber for the stringers.

Be sure that you have a work area large enough to lay out stringers. If you are working indoors, you will need enough room to lay out and cut 16- to 18-foot-long stringers. And you will find this work much easier with a couple of sawhorses on which to rest the stringers.

Treads and Risers. If you are using two-by lumber for the treads, you are usually better off using two or three narrow boards for each tread rather than one wider board. Narrow boards are less likely to cup, and on outdoor

stairs the narrow boards allow you to leave a gap in between that lets dirt and water fall through.

For a more refined-looking stairway, consider using special stair tread stock, which you should be able to find at your local lumberyard. Tread stock is normally sold as 12-inch-wide boards that have been rounded over on one edge for the nosing. The boards can be ripped to the width you need for your own treads. The standard thickness of the boards is $\frac{5}{4}$ (called "five-quarter"), which actually measures about 1 inch for hardwoods and a bit more for softwoods. Yellow pine tread stock is often used on stairs that will be carpeted or painted. It would be an acceptable choice for a basement or other utility staircase. Plywood (1⅛ inches for treads; ¾ inch for risers) is also used for stairs that are going to be carpeted.

Tread stock is also available in oak, mahogany, and other hardwoods. Hardwoods make for more durable and much more attractive stairs. Risers can be made from square-edged boards of the same species of wood. For even stronger stairs, you may be able to find tread and riser stock that has been rabbeted and grooved.

Getting Ready

The step-by-step instructions that follow give techniques for building specific types of stairs in typical situations. The focus is on basic, utility-type stairway designs that homeowners are most likely to build themselves. Before you begin designing and building your stairs, however, read this entire book thoroughly. Although the chapters are organized around different types of stairs, each chapter serves as a further lesson in stairbuilding. The different construction techniques and staircase designs discussed from chapter to chapter are often interchangeable. The next chapter covers the construction of a closed-riser utility staircase. You might want to build this same staircase, however, with open risers, a subject discussed in Chapter 3, page 27.

This book uses terms for specific parts of the stairway that best help to illustrate the simplified approach to stairbuilding taken in these pages. For easy clarification of specialized terms used throughout this book, refer to the Glossary.

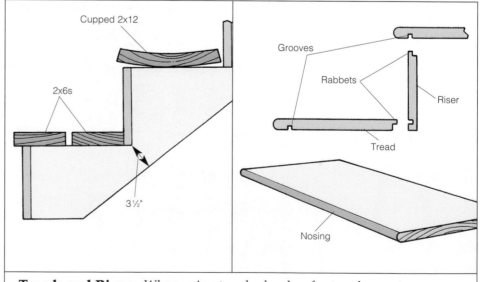

Treads and Risers. When using two-by lumber for treads, use two or three narrower boards rather than one wide board. Building suppliers also carry tread and riser stock milled to interlock.

chapter 2

straight-run stairs

Straight-Run Basics

The closed-riser, notched-stringer set of steps outlined in this chapter is ideal for connecting the basement with the first floor. It is also useful for porches, where closed risers block a view under the porch. For simpler, more basic utility stairs, leave out the risers. (See pages 27 to 32.)

Changing Fractions to Decimals

$\frac{1}{32}$	0.0313
$\frac{1}{16}$	0.0625
$\frac{3}{32}$	0.0938
$\frac{1}{8}$	0.1250
$\frac{5}{32}$	0.1563
$\frac{3}{16}$	0.1875
$\frac{7}{32}$	0.2188
$\frac{1}{4}$	0.2500
$\frac{9}{32}$	0.2813
$\frac{5}{16}$	0.3125
$\frac{11}{32}$	0.3438
$\frac{3}{8}$	0.3750
$\frac{13}{32}$	0.4063
$\frac{7}{16}$	0.4375
$\frac{15}{32}$	0.4688
$\frac{1}{2}$	0.5000
$\frac{17}{32}$	0.5313
$\frac{9}{16}$	0.5625
$\frac{19}{32}$	0.5938
$\frac{5}{8}$	0.6250
$\frac{21}{32}$	0.6563
$\frac{11}{16}$	0.6875
$\frac{23}{32}$	0.7188
$\frac{3}{4}$	0.7500
$\frac{25}{32}$	0.7813
$\frac{13}{16}$	0.8125
$\frac{27}{32}$	0.8438
$\frac{7}{8}$	0.8750
$\frac{29}{32}$	0.9063
$\frac{15}{16}$	0.9375
$\frac{31}{32}$	0.9688
1	1.000

Because a straight-run stairway is longer than any other stairway design, space limitations are the biggest obstacles that you face when building one. If you find you simply don't have the space for a straight-run, you'll have to opt for another style, such as the L-shaped stairway discussed on pages 33 to 42.

Every situation is different. This chapter gives specific dimensions for building a specific stairway. It assumes that you already have a framed stairwell opening. You should study the method used to help you make your own calculations. In most cases, these calculations will result in several choices rather than a single solution. If given a choice, always opt for comfort and safety over meeting minimal standards.

Calculating the Staircase Size

Rise and run, and the relationship between them, are critical features in stair design. "Rise" refers to vertical distance, "run" to horizontal. The "total rise" is the total distance the stairs must climb vertically, while the "total run" is the total distance the stairs cover horizontally. "Unit rise" and "unit run" are layout terms that refer to the dimensions of each individual riser and tread. The rise and run must be nearly identical from step to step. Stairs that vary in tread depth or riser height can be dangerous. Codes require that the difference between the highest and lowest risers not exceed $\frac{3}{8}$ inch. If you do the math in decimals using a calculator and round off to the nearest $\frac{1}{32}$ inch, you'll be close enough. (See "Changing Fractions to Decimals," left.)

1 **Calculating the Total Rise.**
The first task is to determine the total rise. The total rise must be calculated from finished floor surfaces. In this example, the finished floor surfaces are the existing basement slab and the $\frac{3}{4}$-inch hardwood flooring installed over $\frac{3}{4}$-inch plywood

subfloor on the first floor. If you are installing stairs in a house where the finished flooring is not yet in place, find out the flooring thickness, and factor it into the total rise.

To get an exact vertical measurement, set the measuring tape alongside a plumb-bob line. Measure the total rise at each corner of the stairwell opening. If the measurements differ, use the shortest dimension as the total rise, and plan to shim under the stringers when they are installed. In this example, the total rise is $106\frac{3}{4}$ inches.

2 **Calculating the Unit Rise.**
The next task is to calculate the unit rise, which is the height of one step. Codes typically mandate that the maximum step height be $7\frac{3}{4}$ inches, so divide the total rise ($106\frac{3}{4}$) by the legal maximum unit rise ($7\frac{3}{4}$ inches):

$$106.75 \div 7.75 = 13.77$$

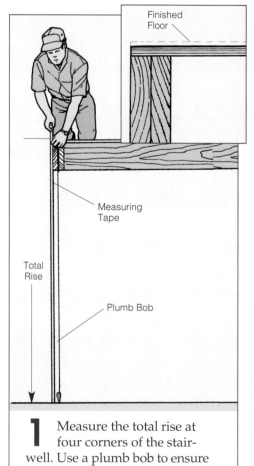

1 Measure the total rise at four corners of the stairwell. Use a plumb bob to ensure that the measuring tape is plumb.

Round this figure up to 14, which is the minimum number of risers the stairs will need. Now divide the total rise by the number of risers to determine the unit rise:

$106.75 \div 14 = 7.625$ ($7\frac{5}{8}$)

To meet most codes, this staircase would require a minimum of 14 risers, each measuring $7\frac{5}{8}$ inches. But many people find a $7\frac{5}{8}$-inch step to be too high. A more comfortable riser height for most people is 7 inches, or even $6\frac{1}{2}$ inches (6 inches should be the minimum for interior stairs). Try adding another riser or two to the formula:

$106.75 \div 15 = 7.117$ ($7\frac{1}{8}$) or

$106.75 \div 16 = 6.672$ ($6\frac{11}{16}$)

Adding one or two risers makes for more-comfortable stairs. Before deciding on the number of risers, however, you need to calculate the unit run and total run, then determine whether you have adequate head-room and landing space.

3 Calculating the Unit Run.
Unit run is the horizontal distance from the face of one riser to the face of the next riser. Codes sometimes refer to the unit run as the tread depth. Building codes require a minimum tread depth of 9 inches. Again, you don't have to build your stairs exactly to this dimension; in fact, 10 or 11 inches is a safer depth.

As a general rule, deeper treads should have shorter risers. Carpenters have developed a variety of formulas for matching tread depth to riser height. Two simple ones are:

rise + run = 17 to 18 and

rise x run = 70 to 75

Using these riser/tread formulas and the target riser dimensions ($7\frac{1}{8}$ inches and $6\frac{11}{16}$ inches), you can calculate the acceptable choices for unit run:

$6\frac{11}{16} + 11 = 17\frac{11}{16}$

$6\frac{11}{16} \times 11 = 73\frac{9}{16}$ or

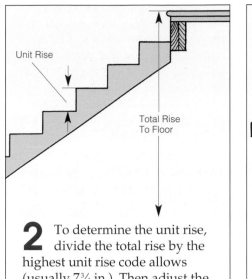

2 To determine the unit rise, divide the total rise by the highest unit rise code allows (usually $7\frac{3}{4}$ in.). Then adjust the rise to suit your preferences.

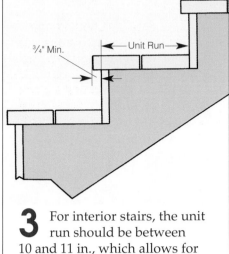

3 For interior stairs, the unit run should be between 10 and 11 in., which allows for the use of two 2x6s per tread with at least a $\frac{3}{4}$-in. nosing.

4 The total run is the distance covered by the stairs. It equals the unit run multiplied by the number of treads.

$7\frac{1}{8} + 10 = 17\frac{1}{8}$

$7\frac{1}{8} \times 10 = 71\frac{1}{4}$

Because all of the results fall within the formula targets, either choice would make for an acceptable and comfortable staircase. For the closed-riser basement stairs we will build in this chapter, the 10-inch tread depth is a good choice because it allows us to use two 2x6s for each tread, thus creating a 1-inch overhang, or nosing.

4 Calculating the Total Run.
Next, multiply the unit run by the total number of treads to reach the total run, which is the horizontal length of the entire staircase.

All stairs have one less tread than riser because the bottom landing, in effect, serves as one tread. So with 15 risers, the staircase has 14 treads, and 14 treads multiplied by the 10-inch unit run equals 140 inches of total run.

5 Checking for Landing Clearance. You may find that the calculated total run leaves insufficient room for a landing. Building codes may require space at both ends of the stairway so that users have a place to enter and exit. Typically, the length of this space, or landing, equals the staircase width; if there will be a door at the top of the staircase that swings toward the stairs, the landing must be at least as long as the door is wide. If you have the space, remember that a bigger landing lets you move larger items up and down the stairs.

The stairwell opening should be positioned to allow enough room for a landing at the top of the stairs.

Use the total run of your stairs to determine whether there's enough landing space at the bottom. Drop a plumb bob from the end of the opening where the top of the stairs will be; mark the floor; and measure out the distance of the total run plus the width of the staircase. If you run into something—a wall, for instance—before you've spanned the total run of the stairs plus the landing, the stairs may not be acceptable by code. Try reducing the unit run, reducing the number of treads (and increasing the unit rise), or both to make the stairs fit in the allotted space; if you still don't have enough room, you'll have to build a different style of staircase.

6 Calculating the Headroom. Knowing where the staircase lands also lets you know whether you can use the stairs without hitting your head on the ceiling. The amount of clear space between the stairs and the ceiling is called headroom, and it's measured vertically from an imaginary sloped plane con-

necting the nosings of each tread. On most stairs, the headroom is shortest just below the header to the stairwell, so check the size of your stairwell opening. Ideally, the total run should equal the length of the stairwell opening. If the opening is significantly shorter than the total run, you may not have sufficient headroom.

To find out exactly how much headroom your run/rise relationship yields, use this formula:

Headroom = [(stairwell length ÷ unit run) x unit rise] - floor thickness

In the example stairs, the stairwell is 133 inches long; the unit run is 10 inches; the unit rise is 7 ⅛ inches, and the floor thickness is 10¾ inches. When plugged into the formula, these figures produce 84 inches of headroom. Typical code requirements say that there must be a minimum of 80 inches (6 feet 8 inches) of headroom in all parts of the stairway. Again, that minimum figure

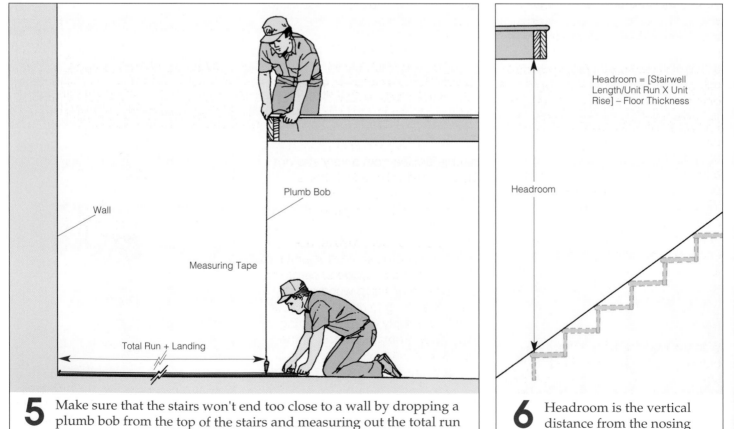

Headroom = [Stairwell Length/Unit Run X Unit Rise] – Floor Thickness

Headroom

Wall

Plumb Bob

Measuring Tape

Total Run + Landing

5 Make sure that the stairs won't end too close to a wall by dropping a plumb bob from the top of the stairs and measuring out the total run plus the landing size.

6 Headroom is the vertical distance from the nosing to any obstruction overhead.

On most stairs, the headroom is shortest just below the header over the bottom steps. If you need a few more inches of headroom to make your stairs conform with the code and all else fails, you can cut the floor or ceiling joists at an angle (the wider the angle, the more space you create). The header is then attached to the joists at the same angle, preferably with metal framing anchors.

If the stairwell has yet to be framed, you can use the total run of the stairs to calculate the stairwell dimensions. A good way to ensure plenty of headroom is to frame the stairwell as long as the total run of the stairs. Often, however, there isn't enough room

for such a large opening. Besides, the minimum headroom clearance is 80 inches, which may let you frame the stairwell shorter.

You can calculate the necessary stairwell length using the formula in "Calculating the Headroom" on page 20. You need to know the unit run, unit rise, and the thickness of the floor through which the stairs pass. By adding the amount of headroom desired to the formula and adjusting it if necessary, you can arrive at an acceptable length. For general purposes, a stairwell that's between 120 inches and 130 inches long usually offers sufficient headroom.

Note that headroom is measured from finished surfaces.

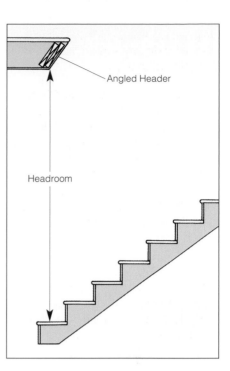

Angled Header

Headroom

is not necessarily ideal. A 6-foot 5-inch resident using such stairs would still feel compelled to duck a bit. Seven feet of headroom is a more comfortable minimal target, and it provides more clearance for moving furniture and other large objects up and down the stairs.

If you find that the headroom is too short, you can adjust the rise and/or run on the stairs or subtract a tread or two to gain a few inches of headroom. For instance, lowering the unit run to 9 ½ inches in the example stairway yields 89 inches of headroom. If you still don't have enough headroom, talk to a carpenter about enlarging the stairwell, or refer to "Making Headroom," above.

Laying Out Stringers

With the unit rise and unit run decided, you can start marking stringers. For stairs up to 40 inches wide, you will need three stringers; wider stairs require additional stringers. You only need to lay out

one stringer, however. Then you can cut it and use it as a template to lay out the others.

1 Making a Story Pole. Because 2x12s are expensive pieces of lumber, it makes sense to take a few extra minutes to double-check your layout. The best way to make sure your dimensions are accurate is to use a story pole. You can make this simple device from a very straight board, preferably a 2x4, that's a few inches taller than the total rise. Mark off the story pole in exact riser increments (7 ⅛ inches in our example). For best results, use dividers set precisely to the unit rise. If you don't have dividers, carefully cut a piece of scrap wood exactly 7 ⅛ inches long to use as a spacer block, or simply use a measuring tape. Start from the bottom of the board and mark off the number of risers in the staircase. Set the story pole in the stairwell, and check that the top mark aligns exactly with the upper-level finished floor. The story pole must be perfectly plumb to get

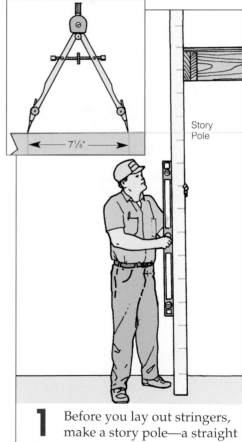

7 ⅛"

Story Pole

1 Before you lay out stringers, make a story pole—a straight board marked with all of the steps in the stairs.

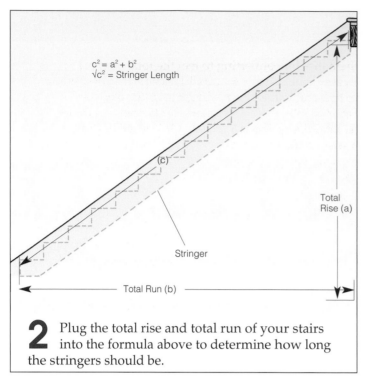

$$c^2 = a^2 + b^2$$
$$\sqrt{c^2} = \text{Stringer Length}$$

(c)

Total Rise (a)

Stringer

Total Run (b)

2 Plug the total rise and total run of your stairs into the formula above to determine how long the stringers should be.

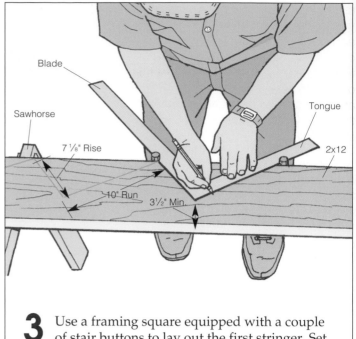

Blade

Sawhorse

Tongue

7 1/8" Rise

10" Run

3 1/2" Min.

2x12

3 Use a framing square equipped with a couple of stair buttons to lay out the first stringer. Set the 2x12 across a pair of sawhorses.

an accurate reading. If the top mark is not within ⅜ inch of the finished-floor height, you will need to recalculate the unit rise.

2 Calculating the Stringer Length. To determine the length of the lumber needed to make the stringers, you need to know the total rise, the total run, and the Pythagorean theorem ($c^2 = a^2 + b^2$). Note that by adding a^2 and b^2 together, you get c^2. You then need to calculate the square root of that figure to find the finished stringer length. Using our example stairs, the results produce a minimal stringer length of 14 feet 8 inches. Dimension lumber is sold in 2-foot increments, so 16-footers would be the shortest you would want to buy. However, a safer length would be 18-footers, which ensures that you'll have enough room to lay out the stringers.

3 Laying Out with a Framing Square. A framing square has a blade (the long, wide end) and a tongue (the short, narrow end). Equipped with a couple of inexpensive stair buttons (or stair gauges), a framing square is the perfect tool for laying out a stringer. Set

one button on the outside edge of the blade at the 10-inch mark (for the tread) and the other button on the outside edge of the tongue at the 7 ⅛-inch mark (for the riser).

Next, sight down the 2x12s to determine whether they are straight or they have a slight arch, or crown, in the middle. Usually, boards are slightly arched in the middle, and you should lay out the stringers so that the crown edge is up. With the stringer lying flat (across a couple of sawhorses is best), place the square as shown so that its corner points away from the wood's crowned edge. Mark along the outside edges of the square; then slide it down the stringer so that it aligns exactly with the previous mark; and mark the next cutout. Number the cutouts as you go along.

4 Dropping the Stringer. The bottom of the stringer needs to be shortened by the thickness of one tread; otherwise, the first step will be too high and the top step too low. On basement stairs and outdoor stairs, the treads are usually two-by or ⁵⁄₄ lumber. Set a scrap piece of tread stock along the bottom cutoff

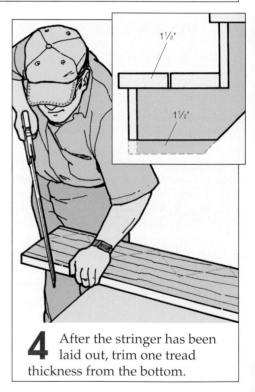

1 1/2"

1 1/2"

4 After the stringer has been laid out, trim one tread thickness from the bottom.

line on the stringer, and draw another line. The stringer should be cut off at this line.

5 Cutting the Stringer. With the stringer laid out, the next step is to cut it. The stringer will then be used as a template to lay out the remaining stringers. For best results, you will need both a circular saw and a handsaw. With the stringer clamped to sawhorses to prevent it from moving, cut it using a circular saw only up to the spot where the tread and riser lines meet. Cutting beyond this point weakens the stringer. Instead, finish the cut using a handsaw.

6 **Checking the Fit.** Set the stringer in the stairwell, with the top of the stringer one riser plus one tread thickness below the finished floor surface. Place a 24-inch level on the tread cutouts to make sure they are at or close to horizontal, and make sure there's enough landing space at the bottom of the stairs. Adjust the stringer up and down slightly until it rests flat against the floor and upper framing. If you can't make the top or bottom rest flat, use a compass open as wide as the gap and draw a line even with the floor or framing, then cut along the line.

7 **Making Other Stringers.** Use the stringer you just cut as a template to lay out the others. Lay the stringer directly on top of another 2x12, and ensure that the edges are perfectly aligned. Be sure that any

Measuring Stringer Length

You can avoid mathematics by converting to feet the total run and total rise of the staircase. Then using the scale 1 foot equals 1 inch, mark on a framing square the total run along the blade and the total rise along the tongue. For example, the total run of this staircase is 11⅔ feet (140 inches), and the total rise is about 8⁹⁄₁₀ feet (106¾ inches). Use a measuring tape to measure the distance between the marks. It comes out to about 15⅛ inches, which when converted back to feet equals about 15 feet 2 inches. (See "Changing Fractions to Decimals," on page 18.)

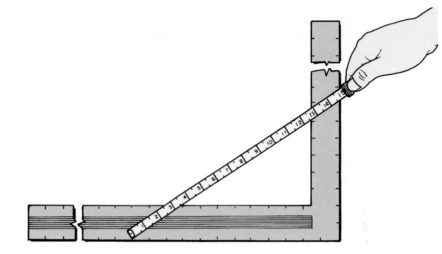

Using the scale 1 in. equals 1 ft., mark on a framing square the total run and total rise, and measure the distance between these points to determine the stringer length.

5 With the stringer resting on sawhorses, use a circular saw to cut just the layout lines. To avoid overcutting the layout, use a handsaw to finish the cut.

6 Set the stringer and check for level treads, adequate landing space, and tight joints. Eliminate gaps by scribing.

2x12 Stringer

Compass to Scribe Bottom

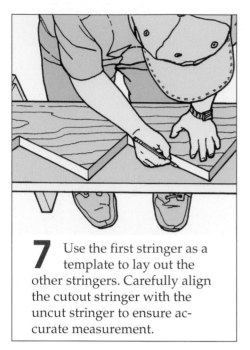

7 Use the first stringer as a template to lay out the other stringers. Carefully align the cutout stringer with the uncut stringer to ensure accurate measurement.

8 With the stringer temporarily in place, trace the outline of a 2x4 onto the bottom of the stringer, and then cut along the lines to make a notch for the kickboard.

crown in the 2x12 will be along the cut edge. Mark and cut out the remaining stringers.

8 Cutting the Kickboard Notch.
The bottom ends of the stringers need to be anchored to the floor. There are several ways to do this, depending on the floor surface. If the stringers are resting on a concrete floor, they should be notched and then attached to a 2x4 kickboard. You can use the kickboard method on a wood floor, too, but it will be easier to attach the stringers

to the floor using angle brackets. (See Step 4, page 25.)

Use a piece of scrap 2x4 to lay out the kickboard notches on each stringer. Cut out the notches with a handsaw or electric saw.

Locating the Stringers

The stringers are installed at the top one riser below the level of the finished floor. The outside stringers should be at least 1½ inches from the edge of the framed opening or

wall framing. This gap allows plenty of room for drywall and a skirtboard.

1 Installing the Hangerboard.
There are several ways to hang the stringers. For indoor stairs, usually the best choice is to nail the stringers to a hangerboard, a piece of ¾-inch plywood that is nailed to the upper framing. Cut the hangerboard two risers wide (about 14 inches) and long enough to fit in the rough opening. Use 8d common nails to secure the hangerboard to the header. An alternative method is to notch the stringers at the top and rest them on a 2x4 ledger.

For deck or porch stairs, the best choices usually are to nail through the rim (or header) joist into the backs of the stringers or to use metal straps or hangers. (See pages 27 to 32 for information on constructing stairs for decks.)

2 Laying Out the Hangerboard.
Measure down from the finished floor surface one unit rise (7⅛ inch in our example) plus the thickness of the tread (1½ inches when using 2x6s) and make a mark on the hangerboard. Then use a 24-inch level to draw a level line at this mark across the hangerboard. The stringers will be installed along this horizontal line.

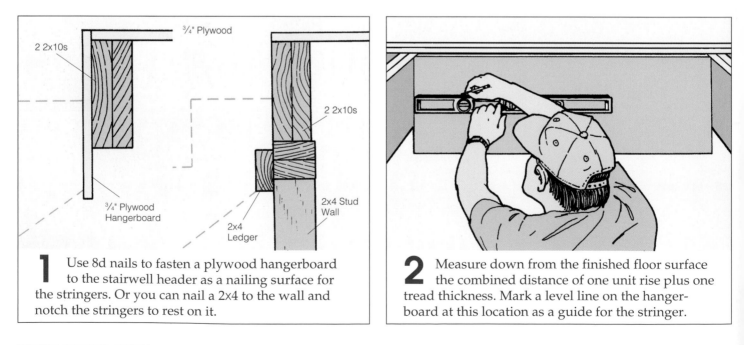

1 Use 8d nails to fasten a plywood hangerboard to the stairwell header as a nailing surface for the stringers. Or you can nail a 2x4 to the wall and notch the stringers to rest on it.

2 Measure down from the finished floor surface the combined distance of one unit rise plus one tread thickness. Mark a level line on the hangerboard at this location as a guide for the stringer.

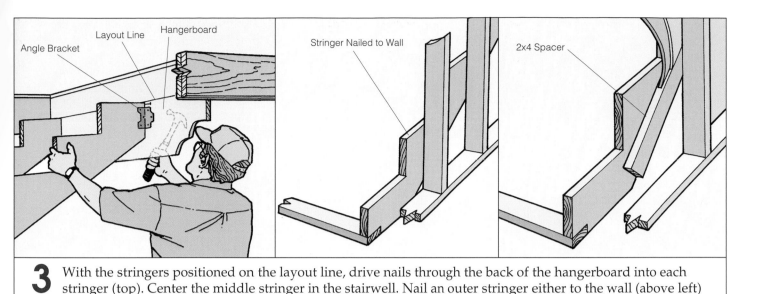

Angle Bracket — Layout Line — Hangerboard

Stringer Nailed to Wall

2x4 Spacer

3 With the stringers positioned on the layout line, drive nails through the back of the hangerboard into each stringer (top). Center the middle stringer in the stairwell. Nail an outer stringer either to the wall (above left) or to a 2x4 spacer (above right).

3 **Installing the Stringers.**
Attach each stringer along the layout line with a single 10d common nail; then check the fit. If there's not enough room for nailing through the back side of the hangerboard and into the stringers, use metal angle brackets to attach the stringers to the hangerboard. The stringers should lie flat against the hangerboard and bear fully on the floor. Place a level across the stringers at each step. If you find a stringer slightly out of alignment, try shimming the bottom. When the stringers are plumb and level, finish nailing.

If you have a wall on one or both sides, you can nail the stringers directly to the wall framing. This makes for a solid connection. If you plan to add drywall and a skirtboard, however, this method would force you to notch the surface material to fit around the stairs. A better solution is to install the stringer away from the wall framing. Leave a space wide enough for the wall covering. A 2x4 makes a good spacer. First, set the stringer in place temporarily, resting against the wall, then draw lines on the studs along the bottom of the stringer. Nail a 2x4 to the studs along this line, then attach the stringer to the spacer. This creates a strong connection and leaves a space for

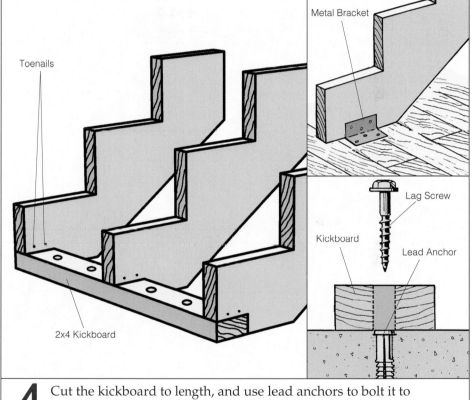

Toenails

2x4 Kickboard

Metal Bracket

Lag Screw

Kickboard

Lead Anchor

4 Cut the kickboard to length, and use lead anchors to bolt it to a concrete floor. Then toenail the stringers to the kickboard. On a wood floor, nail the kickboard or use angle brackets instead of a kickboard.

you to slip in drywall and a skirtboard. The remaining gap will be covered by treads.

If you don't have walls adjacent to the stairs (open stairs), nail the outside stringers to the rough opening framing and through the back of the

hangerboard. The middle stringer should be centered exactly and backnailed through the hangerboard.

4 **Anchoring the Bottom.**
Align the stringers so that they are square to the stairwell header and space them at the bottom to

match the spacing at the top. If you are adding a kickboard, cut a 2x4 to length; then then slip it into the notches and secure it to the floor. The kickboard can be nailed to a wood floor. To attach the kickboard to concrete, use a ½-inch masonry bit (carbide tipped) to drill pilot holes through the kickboard into the concrete. Remove the kickboard; force expandable sleeves into the drilled holes; and then replace the kickboard and insert and tighten 3-inch lag screws.

An alternative method to secure stringers to a wood floor is to screw metal angle brackets to the floor and stringers, as shown.

Finishing the Stairs

Often you aren't overly concerned with the attractiveness of basement stairs. Especially if they will be used less frequently than a primary residential stairway (first to second floor), you may feel satisfied using two-by lumber for the treads, as done in the example

stairs. (For information on alternatives for treads and risers, see "Materials," on page 15.)

1 Installing the Skirtboard.
A skirtboard is a length of hardwood stock—typically 1x12—that is installed on the wall side of the stairs. Although a skirtboard isn't a necessity, it provides protection for the drywall and gives the staircase a finished look. Use a framing square to lay out cut lines at the bottom and top of the skirtboard, and then nail it to the stringer or the wall framing. When the stairs are open on both sides, a skirtboard also improves appearance.

2 Cutting and Installing Treads and Risers. The risers on these stairs are made with 1x8 lumber, which must be ripped (cut in the direction of the wood grain) to $7\frac{1}{8}$ inches in width. Note that the bottom riser is narrower than the others by the thickness of one tread. Cut and install the risers first. Then install the treads, which may be either single 2x12s or two 2x6s. Use 8d finish nails or $2\frac{1}{4}$ inch

flat-head screws, driving two into each stringer (use three fasteners to attach 2x12 treads to each stringer). For a more secure connection, spread construction adhesive along the mating surfaces; then nail or screw them.

The treads on closed-riser stairs must have a nosing between ¾ inch and $1\frac{1}{4}$ inch. For visual balance on open stairs, and to decrease the chance of splitting the treads and risers when fastening them, the sides of both can overhang the stringer.

If one or both sides of the stairway are enclosed, the treads and risers should be cut to fit snugly against the skirtboard. A simple way to get a tight fit is to cut the tread or riser a bit longer than intended. Next, set it in place, and use a compass to scribe a line parallel with the skirtboard. Then cut the tread or riser along this line.

Finishing Touches. The stairs cannot be considered finished until you've installed the railing. See pages 53 to 68 for a complete discussion of railings.

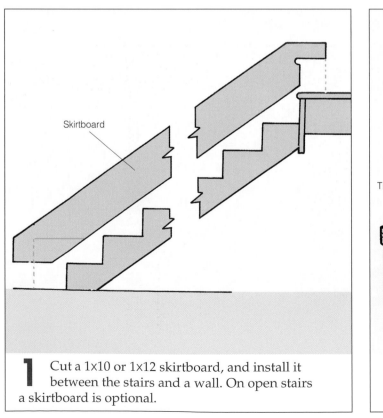

1 Cut a 1x10 or 1x12 skirtboard, and install it between the stairs and a wall. On open stairs a skirtboard is optional.

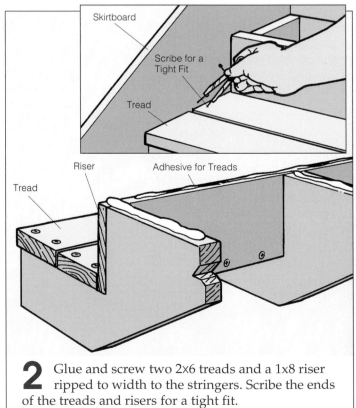

2 Glue and screw two 2x6 treads and a 1x8 riser ripped to width to the stringers. Scribe the ends of the treads and risers for a tight fit.

exterior stairs

Planning the Stairs

Although you could build a short, narrow staircase using only two stringers, most stairs need to be at least 30 inches wide, and stairs that wide should have a third, intermediate stringer. The outside stringers on these stairs may not be notched. Even so, these stringers must be laid out so that you'll know where to install the stair brackets, which are metal angles that support the treads. The middle stringer is notched, and the treads are fastened directly to it.

Be sure to buy the right stair brackets for the treads you plan. The brackets come in different lengths, depending on the tread depth, and some brackets may have more predrilled holes than others, depending on whether they're designed to carry one or two tread boards. If you prefer closed-riser stairs, you can install additional stair brackets to support risers. When building exterior stairs, be sure to use pressure-treated lumber or a decay-resistant wood species.

This chapter will cover all of the steps needed to make open-riser stairs. It will not, however, repeat the detailed discussions of each step that appear on pages 17 to 26.

Calculating Rise and Run

Interior and exterior stairs have the same general dimensional requirements. The minimal standards that define a safe and comfortable stairway are relevant regardless of where the stairs are located. Nevertheless, there are some design differences. Exterior stairs generally aren't constrained by headroom and landing limitations, for example. And exterior stairs generally aren't as steep as interior stairs. Deeper treads, especially, can be a safety feature outdoors when the stairs are wet or covered with snow and ice. For exterior stairs, try to build the stairs

A Notched-Stringer Option

Another common stair style for decks and porches is an open-riser, notched-stringer design. This stairway is similar to the utility stairs discussed in Chapter 2 (page 17), except that it is shorter and doesn't use risers.

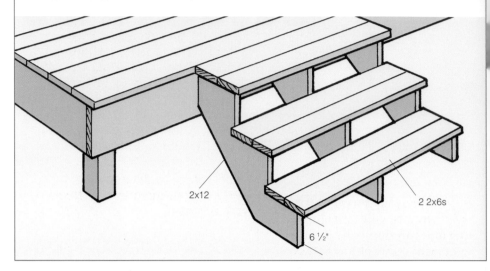

2x12

2 2x6s

6 ½"

with a 6- to 7-inch rise and 11- to 16-inch tread depth. A good choice would be to use two or three 2x6s for each tread. Stair angles are readily available to accommodate this choice, and 2x6s drain better and are less likely to cup or twist than, say, 2x12s.

1 **Finding the Rise.** The total rise is the vertical measurement between finished surfaces. In this case the ground is the bottom finished surface and the deck or porch floor is the top finished surface. If you haven't installed the decking yet,

48-Inch Level

Measuring Tape

1 To minimize errors caused by uneven ground, use a straightedge to extend the deck or porch toward the spot where the stairs will land, and measure the total rise. When the ground slopes across the stairs, codes allow a maximum difference of 1 in. per foot from one end of the bottom step to the other.

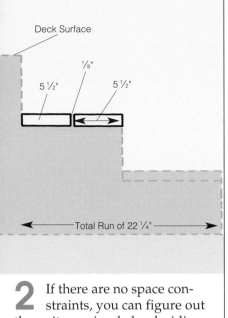

Deck Surface

5 ½"   ⅛"   5 ½"

Total Run of 22 ¼"

2 If there are no space constraints, you can figure out the unit run simply by deciding whether you want to use two or three 2x6s for the tread boards; add the number of treads to get the total run.

be sure to add the thickness of the decking boards to the measurement.

The ground is likely to be uneven. To get an accurate measurement for the total rise, take the measurement from the approximate spot where the stairs will land. This can be done by extending the plane of the decking with a 48-inch level, as shown. In this case, the total rise equals 21 inches.

With a total rise of 21 inches, the only safe choice for the unit rise is 7 inches (21 ÷ 7 = 3 risers). If you tried to build the stairs with more or less risers, the dimensions would be unacceptable.

Sometimes, the ground is sloped perpendicular to the stairs, resulting in a first step that is higher on one side than on the other. Building codes allow this difference in height to be no more than 1 inch per running foot. So if your stairs are 3 feet wide, and the unit rise is 7 inches, you can make one side of the first step 7 inches high and the other side no less than 4 inches high.

2 **Calculating the Run.** If there are no space constraints, you

can feel free to choose the tread depth you want. In this case, the treads are made from two 2x6s, with a ⅛-inch gap between them for drainage. The width of the boards added to the gap yields the tread depth of 11 ⅛ inches.

Find the total run by multiplying the tread depth by the number of treads. Because there is always one less tread than riser, the total run in this example is 22 ¼ inches (2 x 11 ⅛). Measure 22 ¼ inches horizontally from the deck; locate the spot on the ground directly below the 22 ¼-inch mark; then measure the total rise. If it's different from the original measurement, recalculate the unit rise.

Laying Out Stringers

The method for laying out stringers on this type of stairway is a little different from the method used to lay out notched stringers. Here, the framing square establishes lines for the tops of the treads, rather than the bottoms. This keeps the tops of the treads below the top edge of the

stringers, which is more attractive. With the layout line marked, you need only drop down the thickness of the tread to establish the location for the stair angles. This latter line is also the cut line for the middle stringer, which is notched. Using this technique, you do not have to "drop the stringer." Rather, you will have to trim the tops of the stringers flush with the deck surface.

1 **Choosing the Stringer Stock.** To determine the minimal stringer length you will need, use the Pythagorean theorem: Add the squares of the total rise and total run (add one tread depth because the ground acts as the bottom tread), then take the square root of the sum to find the stringer length. Or you can convert the total rise and run to feet, and using the scale 1 foot equals 1 inch, measure across a framing square. (Both the Pythagorean theorem and the framing-square method are described on page 22.) Either way you figure the stringer length, add 6 to 12 inches to allow for waste. Here, the minimal length is 40 inches.

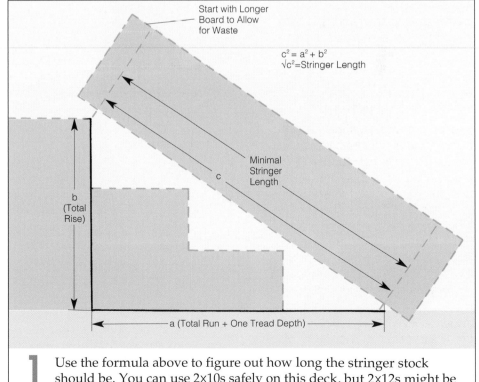

Start with Longer Board to Allow for Waste

$$c^2 = a^2 + b^2$$
$$\sqrt{c^2} = \text{Stringer Length}$$

Minimal Stringer Length

c

b (Total Rise)

a (Total Run + One Tread Depth)

1 Use the formula above to figure out how long the stringer stock should be. You can use 2x10s safely on this deck, but 2x12s might be necessary on a longer staircase.

In this case, 48-inch-long boards would be a good choice.

This staircase can be built safely using 2x10 stringers, but longer or steeper stairs might require 2x12s. If you have any doubts, use the larger stock. Choose lumber that is straight and free of large, loose knots.

2 Laying Out the End Stringers. Use a framing square to lay out the end stringers. Set a stair button on the outside edge of the blade at the tread depth and another on the tongue at the unit rise.

With the stringer lying flat, place the square as shown, with the corner resting on the lumber. Mark along the outside edges of the blade and tongue. Slide the square down the stringer so that it aligns exactly with the previous mark, then lay out the next step. Extend the top riser line to the bottom of the stringer. This will mark your plumb-cut line, where the

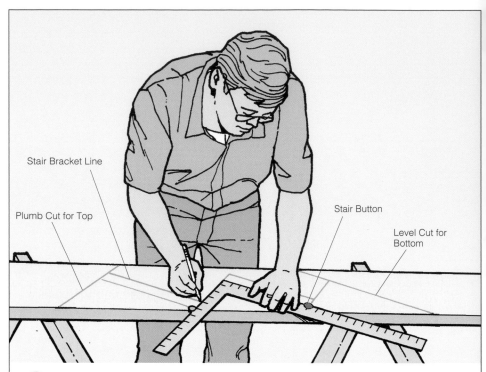

Stair Bracket Line

Plumb Cut for Top

Stair Button

Level Cut for Bottom

2 Set the stair buttons on the framing square and lay out the tops of the treads. Then drop down the thickness of one tread to establish the location of the stair brackets.

Post-and-Pier Anchor

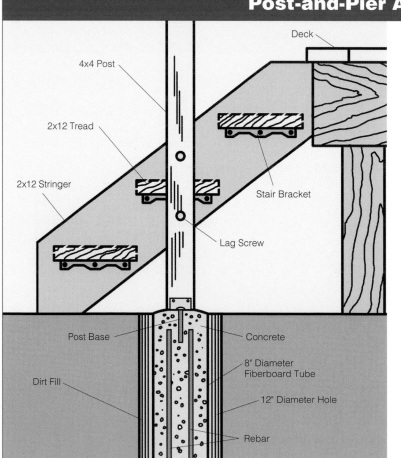

Deck

4x4 Post

2x12 Tread

2x12 Stringer

Stair Bracket

Lag Screw

Post Base

Concrete

8" Diameter Fiberboard Tube

Dirt Fill

12" Diameter Hole

Rebar

A post-and-pier anchor connects the stringers solidly to the ground. The posts serve a double purpose: They provide a connection for the stringers and support the railing.

To prepare the piers, dig 12-inch diameter holes to the frost line. With a handsaw, cut 8-inch fiberboard tubes to reach 2 inches above grade. Keep the tubes plumb while backfilling with dirt taken from the hole. Tamp the dirt with a 2x4 after every 8 inches of fill are added.

Place two #4 L-shaped pieces of rebar in the tube, then fill with a foot of concrete. After a few minutes, lift the rebar 4 inches off the bottom. Fill the tube with concrete. Smooth the top and insert a 4x4 metal post base in the concrete. Position the post bases so that the posts will be square with each other.

When the concrete has cured, attach the 4x4 posts. Lay out the stringers and attach the stair brackets. Attach the stringers to the deck or porch edge, then fasten the stringers to the posts with lag screws.

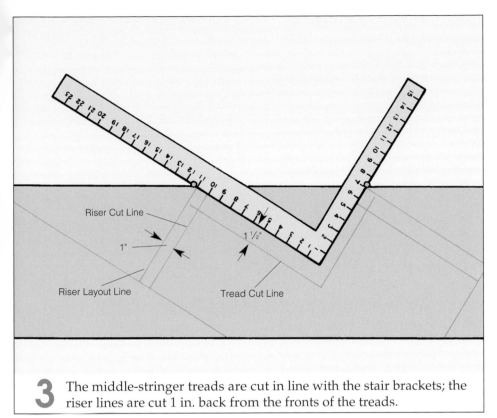

The middle-stringer treads are cut in line with the stair brackets; the riser lines are cut 1 in. back from the fronts of the treads.

with each riser line, 1 inch inside. This will be the riser cut line. Use a circular saw to cut the stringer up to the junction of the rise and run cut lines. Finish cutting using a handsaw.

Assembling the Stairs

The stringers are attached at the top to a rim joist, beam, or other structural member. They can be fastened with metal angle brackets. The bottoms of the stairs must rest on a firm surface, which can be either a bed of gravel or a concrete pad. Or you can build a post-and-pier anchor, as described in "Post-and-Pier Anchor" on page 30.

1 Preparing the Staircase Footing. A 6-inch bed of compacted gravel is the simplest solution for a staircase footing. Dig the hole, then fill it with gravel, tamping the gravel down as you fill. Before installing the stringers, fasten

top end of the stringer butts against the header.

Lay out a tread line along the bottom of the bottom riser, as shown. This marks your level-cut line where the stringer rests on the ground. The tread layout lines indicate the tops of the treads, so the stair brackets must be installed 1½ inches below these lines to support the bottoms of the treads (2x6s being 1½ inches thick). Mark lines 1½ inches below the layout lines. To find each stair-bracket location, measure down from the tread lines the thickness of the treads—1½ inches in this example—and mark lines for the stair brackets.

3 Laying Out the Middle Stringer. The middle stringer is designed so that the riser surface will be recessed 1 inch behind the front end of the treads. With the stair buttons in the same locations, use the framing square to lay out the riser and tread cuts. Follow the directions in the previous step for marking the stair-bracket locations. This will mark the tread cut line on the middle stringer. Then draw a line parallel

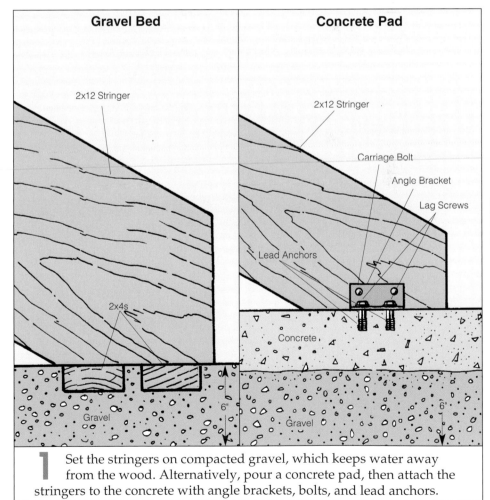

1 Set the stringers on compacted gravel, which keeps water away from the wood. Alternatively, pour a concrete pad, then attach the stringers to the concrete with angle brackets, bolts, and lead anchors.

two 2x4 supports across the bottoms. The supports should be buried in the gravel, helping to distribute the load. For longer life, brush some wood preservative on the bottom ends of the stringers.

Alternatively, you can pour a concrete pad to support the bottom of the stairs. The pad should be at least 4 inches thick and should rest on top of 6 inches of gravel. If the pad will support the treads only, it should be placed at grade, but if you want the pad to act as both a footing and a landing, place it 1½ inches above grade, which allows for water runoff. Fasten the stringers to the concrete with an angle bracket, or angle iron. To attach the angle bracket to the concrete, use a ½-inch carbide-tipped masonry bit to drill pilot holes into the concrete. Force expandable sleeves into the drilled holes; then insert and tighten lag screws. Use ¼-inch carriage bolts to attach the stringers to the angle brackets.

At a minimum, the gravel bed or concrete pad must be big enough to support the stringers. You could make either one bigger to provide a landing at the bottom of the stairs.

2 Attaching Stringers and Treads. Fasten the stair brackets to the stringers using the screws specifically recommended by the manufacturer.

Use metal framing angles to attach the stringers to a rim joist, beam, or other structural member. Position the stringer so that the top of the first tread is one unit rise below the deck or porch. You may have to trim the tops of the stringers before hanging them. Space the end stringers as far apart as the treads will be wide (36 inches is a good target).

Fasten the middle stringer with framing angles, centered between the end stringers. The top of the middle stringer should align with the stair brackets on the end stringers. If the rim joist or header doesn't offer enough nailing surface to attach the middle stringer, try attaching the stringer with metal strapping, or nail the stringer to a hangerboard made of exterior-grade plywood. If you use a hangerboard, don't forget to trim ¾ inch from the back end of the stringer to compensate for the plywood thickness.

Each tread on this staircase is made up of two 2x6s. Cut the treads to length. Using the fasteners recommended by the stair-bracket manufacturer, attach the first tread so that it is flush with or slightly below the tops of the end stringers. Use a 16d nail to establish a ⅛-inch gap between the tread pieces. If you think you won't have enough clearance between the ground and the first tread to drive screws, consider installing the first tread before attaching the stringers to the rim joist.

Codes generally require a handrail if the staircase contains three or more risers. See pages 53 to 68 for a complete discussion of railings.

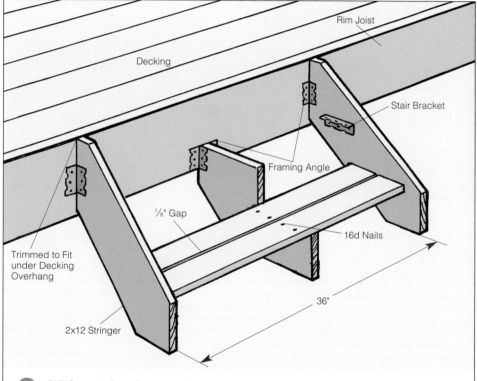

2 With stair brackets in place, attach the tops of the stringers to a structural member. Cut the treads and screw them to the brackets. If you can't get access to the brackets from below the treads, consider installing the treads before fastening the stringers to the porch or deck.

chapter 4

L-shaped stairs

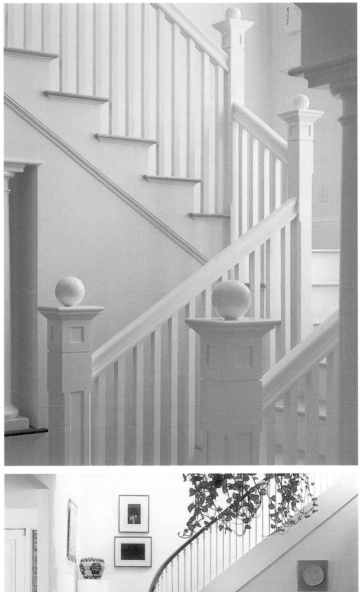

About L-Shaped Stairs

Even if space isn't a factor, many people find L-shaped stairs to be more appealing than straight-run stairs. By turning the corner at 90 degrees, the L-shaped staircase breaks the direct visual line from top to bottom. If the landing can be equipped with a small window, the effect will be even more pleasing. Also, a landing installed midway between the upper and lower floors provides a convenient rest spot for those who have difficulty getting up and down stairs.

The L-shaped stairway with a landing is essentially nothing more than two straight-run stairs heading in perpendicular directions. In terms of calculating dimensions, treat the landing as just another tread.

The staircase in this chapter is a closed-riser model, with standard hardwood tread stock and matching hardwood risers. The landing can be covered with ¾-inch hardwood flooring installed over a ¾-inch plywood subfloor. Oak is the most popular hardwood for stairs, but other woods could be used as well. If you were building these stairs for utility purposes only and wanted to cut costs, you could use two-by lumber for the treads and leave out the risers. Be sure to adjust dimensions to your design variations.

Calculating Rise and Run

Treads and risers on an L-shaped stairway must meet the same minimal requirements as on straight-run stairs. It is essential that tread depth and riser height be identical on both the upper and lower staircase runs.

1 **Calculating the Rise.** The total rise is the vertical distance between finished floors. In this case, the upper and lower floors will be finished with identical material (¾-inch hardwood flooring or ½-inch carpet). The total rise measures 105 inches. Divide the total rise by 7¾ inches (maximum riser height) to find the minimum number of risers the stairway will require. The result is 14 (rounded up from 13½).

Divide the total rise (105 inches) by 14 risers to find the unit rise (7½ inches). The stairway could be built with 15 7-inch risers (15 x 7 = 105), but using 14 risers allows the landing to be located exactly halfway between the floors. As long as you're not constrained by a wall, it's easiest to build the landing halfway between floors because the stringers will then be identical for both flights of stairs. If a wall limits the amount of space you have to build stairs. (See "Limited Total Run" on page 35.)

2 **Calculating the Landing Height.** Divide the total number of risers in half (14 ÷ 2 = 7), then multiply the result by the riser height (7 x 7½ = 52½). This establishes that the finished height of the landing should be 52½ inches. Because the landing will be covered with ¾-inch plywood and ¾-inch hardwood, subtract the combined thickness of these flooring materials from the landing height to find the framing height (52½ – 1½ = 51 inches).

3 **Determining the Landing Size.** The finished landing on an L-shaped staircase should be square, with the sides equal to the width of the treads. However, the stringers for the upper section will rest on the landing, so you need to frame the landing larger than its finished size. The side of the frame to which the lower stringers will be attached

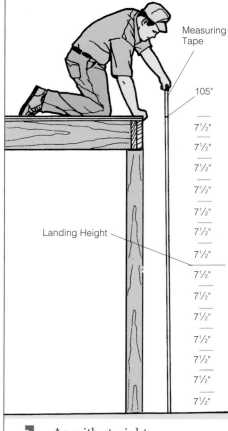

Measuring Tape

105"

7½"
7½"
7½"
7½"
7½"
7½"
7½"
7½"
7½"
7½"
7½"
7½"
7½"
7½"

Landing Height

1 As with straight-run stairs, begin planning an L-shaped staircase by finding the total rise. Be sure that your measurement is from finished floor to finished floor.

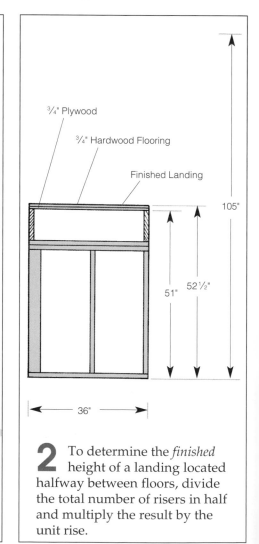

¾" Plywood

¾" Hardwood Flooring

Finished Landing

105"

51" 52½"

36"

2 To determine the *finished* height of a landing located halfway between floors, divide the total number of risers in half and multiply the result by the unit rise.

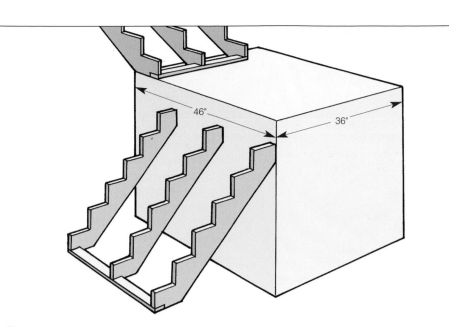

3 Because stringers to the upper stairway rest on the landing, the framed platform must be larger than the finished landing surface.

should be built about 1 unit run longer than the other side, which will be framed to the length of the treads. In this case, the frame measures 36 inches by 46 inches because the unit run is 10 inches, as described in Step 4, below.

4 **Finding the Run.** To determine the unit run, use the run-to-rise formulas explained on page 19:

unit rise + unit run = 17–18

unit rise x unit run = 70–75

By applying the unit rise (7½ inches) to these formulas, you will find that 10 inches is a good unit run.

Next, find the total run for the upper stairs. Because there are seven risers, there will be six treads.

Limited Total Run

Sometimes, you need to install an L-shaped staircase because there isn't enough space for straight-run stairs. Maybe the stairs face a wall, or maybe a straight-run would extend into a hallway. In any event, the problem you face is that the total run is too short to put in straight-run stairs. So you need a landing for an L-shaped stairway, and the landing must be built in a particular spot, whether it's against a wall opposite the stairwell header or flush with a wall on one side of a hallway. Because the landing's location is fixed, its height will be determined by the number of steps needed to reach it.

First, figure out the total rise and the unit rise. For this example, 105 inches of total rise yields 7½ inches of unit rise. Then measure the total run available for the upper staircase. You must subtract the size of the landing from the total run, then occupy the leftover space with treads.

If the total run for the upper staircase is 86 inches, for example, and the stairs are 36 inches wide, then the finished landing will be 36 inches square, and the space you have left over is 50 inches. If you will use a hangerboard to connect the stringers to the header, subtract ¾ inch from the total run. You need to fill the 50-inch space with treads. Having already determined that the unit rise will be 7½ inches, you must find a unit run that will fill the space and fall within the limitations set by the run-to-rise formulas. In this case, five 10-inch-deep treads work out perfectly. Because

there's always one more riser than tread, you'll need six risers, each 7½ inches high, putting the finished landing surface 45 inches below the upper finished floor. Measure down from the upper finished floor 45 inches, and use a level and straightedge, line level, or water level to transfer this height to the landing area. Then build the landing as described in "Framing the Landing" on page 36.

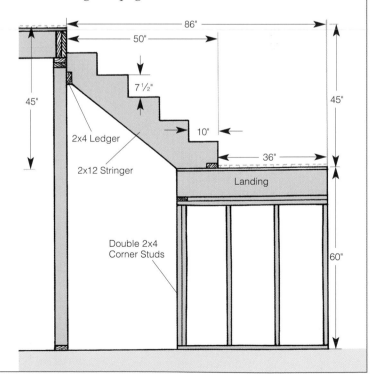

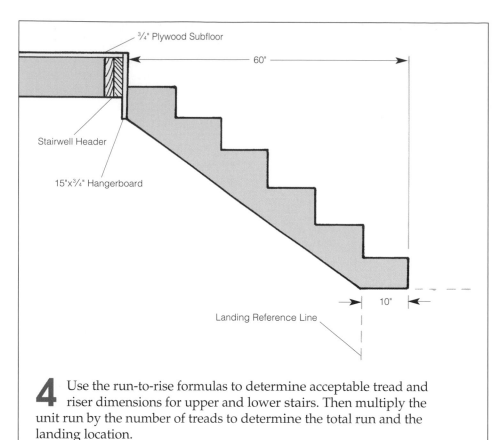

¾" Plywood Subfloor

60"

Stairwell Header

15"x¾" Hangerboard

10"

Landing Reference Line

1 **Attaching Joists to the Wall.**
Mark the height of the landing framing (51 inches) on one wall stud; then use a level to mark the rest of the studs. Nail a 46-inch-long 2x10 joist to the studs, even with the layout marks. Then nail a 33-inch-long joist at the same height on the adjacent wall.

2 **Framing the Landing Walls.**
The short walls that support the landing are framed like normal stud walls, with a bottom plate and a double top plate. Measure the distance from the floor to the bottom edge of the joists. If you used 2x10s at a 51-inch height, the distance should be 41¾ inches, but measure to be sure. This is the height of the landing wall.

Now subtract 4½ inches from this figure (the thickness of the three plates) to find the stud length (38¼ inches here). Cut eight 2x4s to this length. Attach studs to the bottom and top

4 Use the run-to-rise formulas to determine acceptable tread and riser dimensions for upper and lower stairs. Then multiply the unit run by the number of treads to determine the total run and the landing location.

Multiply the number of treads by the tread depth to find the total run (6 x 10 = 60 inches). The bottom riser will be located 60 inches from the hangerboard, measured horizontally. Use the same dimensions for the lower flight of stairs.

Framing the Landing

Typically, a landing on an L-shaped staircase is encased by walls on two sides. Joists for these sides can be nailed directly to the wall studs. The other two sides of the landing need to be framed using standard 2x4 framing techniques.

If the walls are covered with drywall, you need to locate the wall studs so that the joists can be nailed to them. If necessary, the entire landing can be set on three framed walls (if only one side abuts a wall) or four framed walls in case no side abuts a wall. If your landing is a different size from this one, be sure that the studs and joists in the framing are located 16 inches on center.

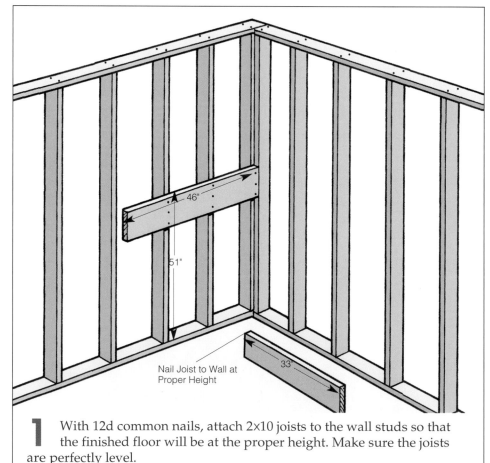

46"

51"

33

Nail Joist to Wall at Proper Height

1 With 12d common nails, attach 2x10 joists to the wall studs so that the finished floor will be at the proper height. Make sure the joists are perfectly level.

plates as shown, spaced no more than 16 inches apart.

Cut to length the two double top plates (42½ inches and 36 inches); then attach them to the top plates using 8d nails. The double top plate on the short wall should overlap the end of the wall 3½ inches; the double top plate on the long wall should stop 3½ inches from the end of the wall. Fit each wall under the end of the perimeter joist as shown, and secure the walls to the house framing and floor. Make sure the landing frame is square with the adjacent walls; then use 10d nails to fasten the landing walls together through the top plates and the corner joists.

Attach the other two perimeter joists along the tops of the landing walls. Toenail the joists to the top plate. Measure the distance between the joists (43 inches here). Cut and install the intermediate joist using joist hangers.

3 **Installing the Landing Subfloor.** Cut a piece of ¾-inch plywood that is flush with the landing on three sides and overhangs the long side by ¾ inch. The overhang will cover the hangerboard. Notch the overhang so that it extends only as far as the outside stringer, as shown. Apply construction adhesive on the joist tops before using 8d common nails to fasten the subfloor to the joists.

Making the Stringers

You need to make a total of six stringers. If your landing is located exactly midway between the upper and lower floors (as in this example), and you will use the same flooring material for both floors and the landing, then all stringers will be identical. They will be attached to hangerboards at the tops and rest on kickboards at the bottoms. Lay out and cut one stringer; then use it as a template to lay out the others.

1 **Choosing the Stringer Stock.** The stringers are made with 2x12 stock. To determine the minimum length for each one, use the Pythagorean theorem and the figures for total rise and total run on each section, as shown. Be sure to add one unit run to the total run in your calculations. Or you could convert the total rise and run to feet, and using the scale 1 foot equals 1 inch,

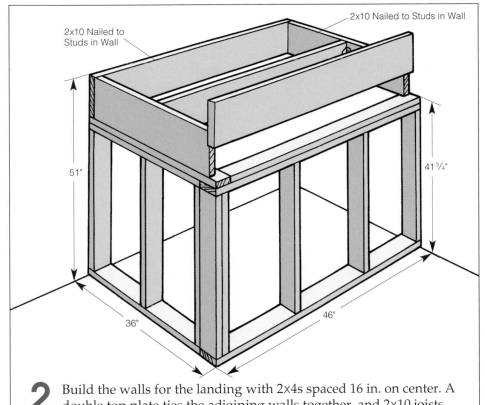

2 Build the walls for the landing with 2x4s spaced 16 in. on center. A double top plate ties the adjoining walls together, and 2x10 joists bear on the top plates.

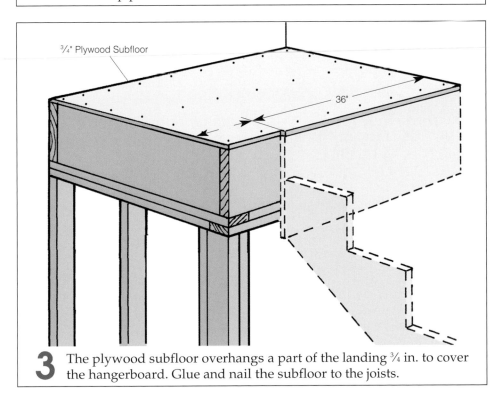

3 The plywood subfloor overhangs a part of the landing ¾ in. to cover the hangerboard. Glue and nail the subfloor to the joists.

mark these points on a framing square. Then measure the distance between these points to find the length of the stringers.

The result in the drawing is a minimal length of 88 inches for each of the six stringers. You could cut stringers from 8-foot 2x12s as long as the ends of the lumber are free of splits. Choose lumber for the stringers that is straight and free of large, loose knots.

2 Laying Out and Cutting the Stringers.
Use a framing square to lay out the stringers. Set a stair button on the outside edge of the blade to the unit run (10 inches) and another on the tongue to the unit rise (7½ inches).

With the stringer lying flat, place the square as shown, with the corner resting on the lumber. Mark along the outside edges of the framing square. Slide the square down the stringer so that it aligns exactly with the previous mark, then lay out the next cutout. Extend the top rise line to the bottom of the stringer. This will mark your plumb-cut line.

3 Dropping the Stringer.
Usually, "dropping the stringer" is a simple matter of trimming the thickness of a tread from the bottom of the stringer. In this case, however, the tread stock is thicker than the hardwood flooring, which is not yet in place. So the bottoms of the stringers need to be shortened by the thickness of a tread minus the thickness of the finished flooring. The treads on this staircase will be ⁵⁄₄-inch hardwood, which is 1⅛ inches thick, and the flooring will be ¾ inch thick. The difference between the two materials is ⅜ inch, and this is the amount to drop the stringers. Draw a line ⅜ inch from the bottom of each stringer, and cut along the line.

Keep in mind the type of finished flooring you will install before you drop the stringers; sometimes the upper stringers must be dropped a different amount from the lower

stringers. For example, if the stringers will rest on a basement slab, they must be dropped the full thickness of the treads, or 1⅛ inches. The upper stringers, however, may need to be dropped only ⅜ inch. When sets of stringers need to be dropped different amounts, you will need to make two

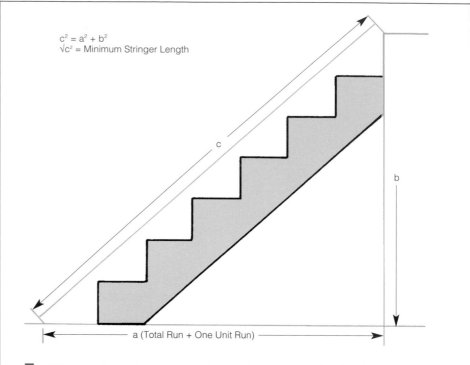

$$c^2 = a^2 + b^2$$
$$\sqrt{c^2} = \text{Minimum Stringer Length}$$

c

b

a (Total Run + One Unit Run)

1 Use the formula above to determine the length of stringer stock you need. Use only straight, solid boards for stringers.

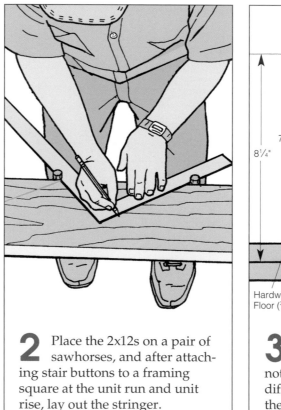

2 Place the 2x12s on a pair of sawhorses, and after attaching stair buttons to a framing square at the unit run and unit rise, lay out the stringer.

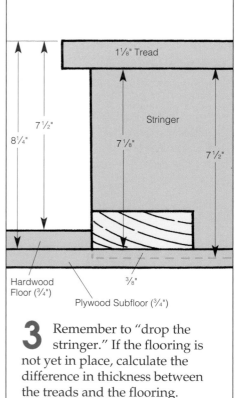

1⅛" Tread

7½"

8¼"

Stringer

7⅛"

7½"

Hardwood Floor (¾")

⅜"

Plywood Subfloor (¾")

3 Remember to "drop the stringer." If the flooring is not yet in place, calculate the difference in thickness between the treads and the flooring.

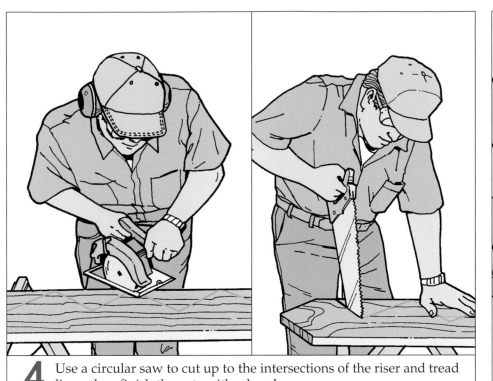

4 Use a circular saw to cut up to the intersections of the riser and tread lines, then finish the cuts with a handsaw.

5 Cut notches in the stringers for the 2×4 kickboard.

templates: one for the upper stringers, one for the lower stringers.

4 **Cutting the Stringer.** Use a circular saw to cut the stringer up to the junction of the rise and run layout lines. Finish cutting using a handsaw. Use the cut-out stringer as a template to lay out the others.

5 **Cutting Notches for Kickboards.** The bottom of the stringers will rest on 2x4 kickboards to anchor them to the lower floor and the landing. Use a piece of scrap 2x4 to lay out the notches on each stringer. Cut out the notches using a handsaw or electric saw.

Assembling the Stairs

The stringers are installed one riser plus one tread thickness below the finished flooring of both the landing and the upper floor. The stringers will be attached to hangerboards at the top and a kickboard at the bottom.

1 **Installing the Hangerboards.** A hangerboard is a piece of ¾-inch plywood that is nailed to the stairwell header and the landing.

Cut both hangerboards two risers high (about 15 inches) and wide enough to span the stairwell opening at the top of the stairs. The bottom hangerboard should be just

wide enough to provide a nailing surface for the outer stringers. Use 8d common nails to nail the hangerboards securely to the joists. Think about the finished ceiling now. If the

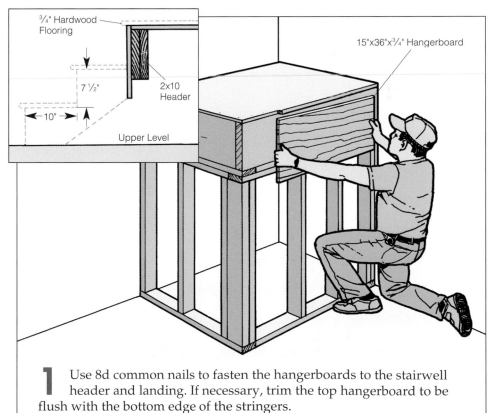

¾" Hardwood Flooring

7 ½"

2x10 Header

10"

Upper Level

15"x36"x¾" Hangerboard

1 Use 8d common nails to fasten the hangerboards to the stairwell header and landing. If necessary, trim the top hangerboard to be flush with the bottom edge of the stringers.

hangerboard will interfere with the ceiling drywall, trim the hangerboard so that it will be flush with the bottom edges of the stringers.

2 Setting the Stringers. On each hangerboard, measure down from the finished floor surface one unit rise (7½ inches in our example) plus the thickness of the tread (1⅛ inches here), and mark a layout line on the hangerboard.

Attach each stringer along the layout line with a single nail, then check the fit. The stringers should lie flat against the hangerboard and be perfectly level with the floor. Place a level across the stringers at each step. If you find one stringer slightly out of alignment, shim the bottom level with the others.

3 Attaching Spacers to Walls. If you have a wall on one or both sides, you can nail the stringers directly to the wall framing. If you plan to add drywall and a skirtboard, however, leave a space wide enough for both between the wall and the stringer. Use a 2x4 spacer for this purpose. Position the stringer even with the layout line on the hangerboard. Check that the stringer butts tightly against both the hangerboard and the floor. Then mark the bottom edge of the stringer on the wall, and cut a 2x4 to fit along this line. Remove the stringer; spike the 2x4 spacer to the wall with 16d nails; then reset the stringer and nail it to the 2x4 spacer using16d nails.

4 Attaching the Stringers. Drive 12d nails through the back of the hangerboard into the stringers. If the framing on the landing pre-vents this, attach the stringers to the hangerboards using metal angle brackets. Attach the middle stringer so that it is centered between the outside stringers.

Make sure that the stringers are square to the landing and the

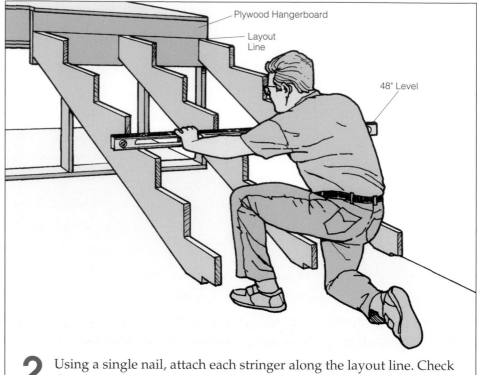

2 Using a single nail, attach each stringer along the layout line. Check that the stringers are level and straight before you finish nailing.

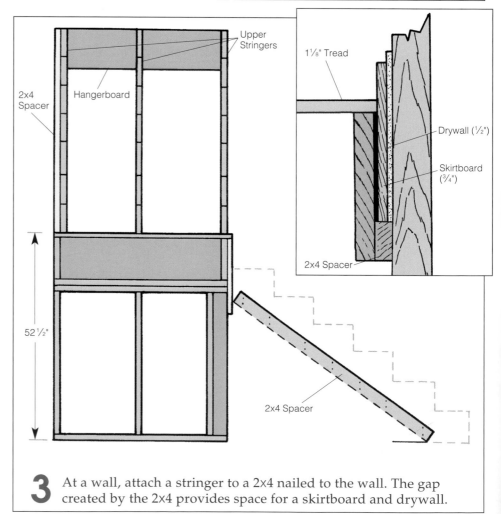

3 At a wall, attach a stringer to a 2x4 nailed to the wall. The gap created by the 2x4 provides space for a skirtboard and drywall.

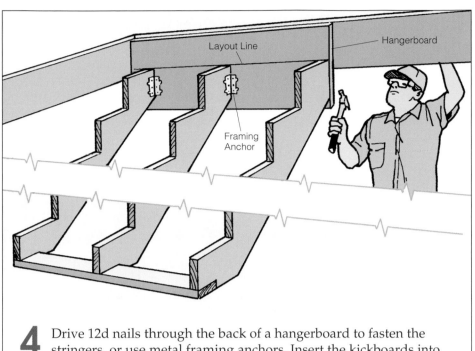

Drive 12d nails through the back of a hangerboard to fasten the stringers, or use metal framing anchors. Insert the kickboards into the notches at the bottoms of the stringers, and nail everything together.

Finishing the Stairs

If you were building a utility staircase, such as to the basement, you might be content to use two-by lumber for the treads and one-by pine for the risers. The stairs in this chapter, however, have been designed to take 1 1/8-inch hardwood treads, which are cut from standard tread stock available at lumberyards and building-supply outlets. Usually, the nosing on the tread stock is already rounded over, but you need to cut the boards to the right length and width before installing them. The risers and skirtboard could be made from the same type of wood, using 3/4-inch boards.

1 Cutting and Installing Treads and Risers. To minimize squeaks, the treads should be attached to the stringers with screws and construction adhesive spread along all mating surfaces. Drill pilot holes before driving screws. The risers can be attached using 6d nails

stairwell framing, and that they are properly spaced at the bottom. Cut a 2x4 kickboard to length; slip it into the notches in the stringers; then

secure the kickboard to the floor and the stringers to the kickboard. This will help keep the stringers from shifting.

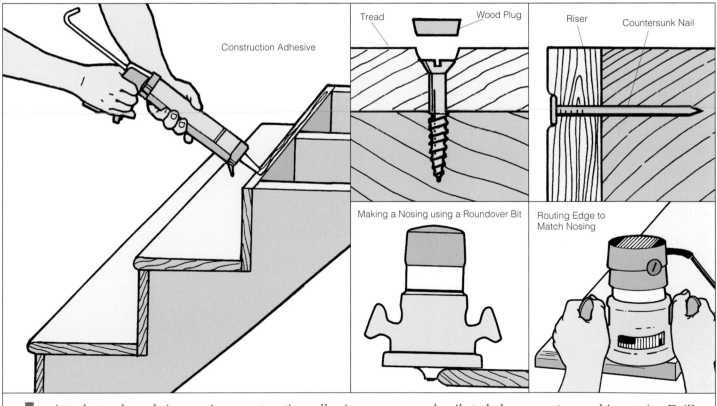

1 Attach treads and risers using construction adhesive, screws, and nails to help prevent squeaking stairs. Drill pilot and countersink holes, and cover them with wood plugs. If the treads will overhang the sides of the stairs, shape the tread ends using a roundover bit in a router.

and construction adhesive. Use wood screws to fasten the bottoms of the risers to the back edges of the treads, too. If you are using hardwood treads and risers, you will probably want to cover the heads of the screws and nails for a neater appearance. Countersink the screws, then cover them with wood plugs that match the tread stock. You can buy wood plugs at home centers and lumberyards. On the risers, use a nail set to drive the heads of the nails below the surface, then plug the holes with matching putty. Sand or plane the surfaces flush.

The treads must be at least 36 inches wide. If you are using hardwood tread stock and you want the treads to overhang the side a bit, you might want to shape the tread ends to match the rounded nosing. Use a router fitted with a roundover bit to shape the ends, as shown. You will need to round over both the top and bottom. Use sandpaper to remove any burn marks on the end grain.

Cut and install the bottom riser first. It must be ripped to match the height of the stringer. Note that it is narrower than the other risers by the thickness of a tread. Then cut and install the second riser before installing the first tread. Install the third riser, followed by the second tread, and continue up the stairway. If the skirtboard is already in place, you can cut both the treads and risers to butt tightly against the skirt.

The easiest way to get a perfect fit is to position the riser or tread tightly against the skirtboard, and then use

a compass to scribe the exact shape of the skirtboard on the end of the tread. If you need to install a skirtboard on an open side, use a framing square to lay out cut lines at the bottom and top, then nail the skirtboard to the stringer.

The treads on a closed-riser staircase must have a nosing between ¾ inch and 1¼ inch.

2 Attaching the Angle Blocks.
Another way to prevent squeaky stairs is to install angle blocks. Cut

the triangular blocks out of scrap two-by lumber, then attach them with adhesive and nails to the underside of the stairs at the junction where the tread meets the riser. Attach two or three angle blocks at each stair.

If you've taken the trouble to install attractive hardwood treads and risers on the stairs, you will want to be equally committed to installing a matching railing. You'll find some ideas on making your own balustrade and handrail or installing a prefabricated railing on pages 53 to 68.

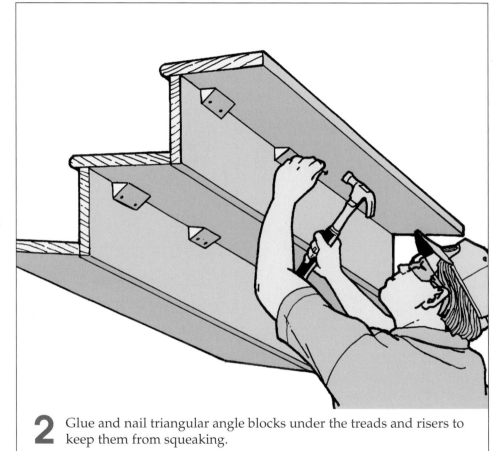

2 Glue and nail triangular angle blocks under the treads and risers to keep them from squeaking.

a three-step winder

Winder Pros and Cons

Winders are not as safe as straight-run stairs or stairs with a landing. Use a winder only if you have no other choice. For one thing, the irregularly shaped treads present a hazard. An important component of stairway safety is ensuring that the movement from step to step is routine and re-petitive. By their nature, winders require users to adjust their routine as they move around the corner. Also, users who try to climb the stairs using the narrow section of the winder may find insufficient support for their feet. Finally, while a landing is likely to break a fall down the stairs, winder stairs would not.

Restrictions. Winders are often closely regulated by codes. In some areas you may not be allowed to build a winder as the main stairway in a house. Many codes won't allow winders in which the treads come to a point. Instead, treads are required to be at least 10 inches deep along the "line of travel," usually defined as the line running 12 inches from the narrow edge of the treads.

Some codes additionally stipulate that the minimum width of treads be no less than 6 inches at any point. A continuous handrail is required along the side with the narrower treads. Be sure to check your local code carefully.

Saving Space. A winder introduces a shortcut in the line of travel, similar to cutting across a corner lot rather than following the sidewalk. The reduced impact on the floor plan is most apparent when the winder treads come to a point, as shown in the drawing. When space is too limited even for a winder, you may have to consider spiral stairs. (See page 51 for details.)

Building a Basic Winder

As with all stairs, you need to find the total rise, then calculate a comfortable unit rise and unit run. To better illustrate the differences between stairs with winders and stairs with a landing, the following instructions will assume the same total rise (105 inches) and number of risers (14) as the L-shaped stairs in Chapter 4. Be sure to read pages 33–42 carefully before attempting to build a winder.

You need to frame a landing and build two sets of stringers. The differences here are that one set of stringers is reduced by two treads, whose place will be taken by the two winder steps you will install on top of the landing. Also, the upper stringers won't rest on the landing. Instead, they are hung with joist hangers off the side of the top winder step. This allows you to build a smaller frame.

1 Building the Landing. Two sides of the 36-inch by 36-inch landing rest on short framed walls. The joists for the other two sides are attached directly to the house framing. If your landing is freestanding (that is, not adjacent to walls), you can frame short walls to support the other two sides. In the example stairs, the landing serves as the fifth tread from the bottom, and the total height of the landing is 37 ½ inches (using a unit rise of 7 ½ inches). Use construction adhesive and 8d common nails to install the landing subfloor.

2 Laying Out the Winders. Use a 36 x 36-inch piece of ¾-inch plywood to lay out the winders. Lay out three treads so that the tread width along the line of travel (usually 12 inches from the narrow end of the

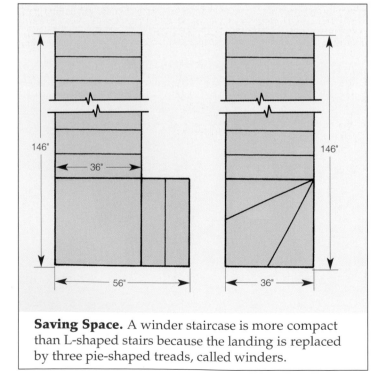

Saving Space. A winder staircase is more compact than L-shaped stairs because the landing is replaced by three pie-shaped treads, called winders.

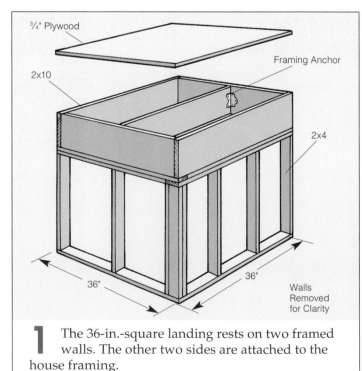

1 The 36-in.-square landing rests on two framed walls. The other two sides are attached to the house framing.

treads) is equal on each tread. An easy way to ensure this is to draw a diagonal line on the landing, as shown. Measure in from each corner 18¾ inches, and mark these spots on the diagonal line. Then draw a line from the inside corner of the plywood through each of the two marks. This divides the plywood into three pie-shaped wedges. Each wedge serves as a layout for one tread.

Note that this 18¾-inch dimension is good only on a 36 x 36-inch landing. For a larger landing, the dimension is larger. For example, for a 40 x 40-inch landing, the dimension is 20¾ inches. For other sizes, you can experiment with the layout until the tread width along the line of travel is equal from step to step.

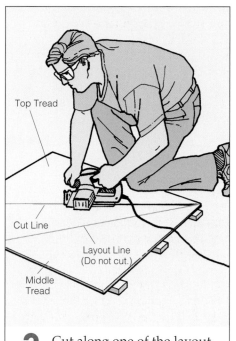

2 Draw a diagonal line and measure 18¾ in. from each corner. Then draw lines from an adjacent corner through the 18¾-in. marks just made.

3 Cut along one of the layout lines only. Each of the resulting two pieces will serve as a tread.

3 Cutting the Treads. Cut out one of the treads. This piece will be the top tread, and the remaining two-thirds piece will be the middle tread. The landing itself will serve as the bottom tread.

4 Building the Winders. You need to build frames for the top two steps of the three-step winder. The unit rise on this example staircase is 7½ inches. From this dimension, subtract the thickness of the plywood treads (¾ inch). The result, 6¾ inches, is the height of each frame. Rip several 2x8s to 6¾ inches; then cut and assemble the frames using 10d nails.

5 Assembling the Winder. Keeping the sides flush, toenail the larger of the two frames to the landing. For extra holding power, use 8d ring-shank nails and make sure that the toenails are driven firmly into the frame. Then nail the larger plywood tread to the frame.

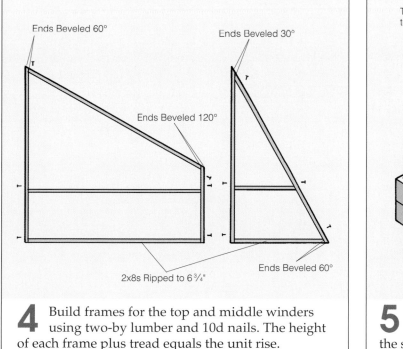

4 Build frames for the top and middle winders using two-by lumber and 10d nails. The height of each frame plus tread equals the unit rise.

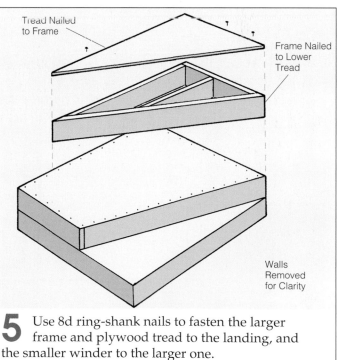

5 Use 8d ring-shank nails to fasten the larger frame and plywood tread to the landing, and the smaller winder to the larger one.

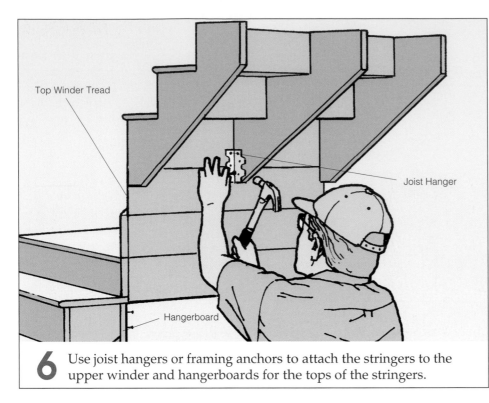

You will need to "drop the stringer" on the lower stringers. Both sets of stringers can be attached at the top with hangerboards.

6 Use joist hangers or framing anchors to attach the stringers to the upper winder and hangerboards for the tops of the stringers.

Adding Nosings

With the winder stairs built and the stringers cut and attached, you can now cut and install the remaining treads and risers, using ¾-inch plywood. If the stairs are going to be carpeted, you may not have to include a nosing on the treads. (Check your local code.)

If you need to add a nosing for carpeted stairs, cut the treads accordingly. You can add nosings to the winder treads with half-round molding, which is available in a variety of sizes. Cut the molding to the width of the tread; apply construction adhesive or glue to the mating surfaces; and then drive 4d or 6d finishing nails through the molding and into the winder.

If the winder treads are going to be covered with hardwood, you don't need to worry about the nosing at this stage. Instead, the finish treads—with one edge bullnosed for the nosing—can be cut to allow for the proper overhang.

Finally, fasten the smaller riser frame and tread.

6 **Installing the Stringers.** The stringers are cut and installed much like those in the previous chapter. The one difference is that the stringers for the upper staircase section do not rest on the platform. Rather, they are hung from the back side of the upper riser with joist hangers. Do not "drop the stringer" in this case. Instead, clip off a flat edge on the stringer bottoms so that they can rest in the joist hangers. If the end stringers are flush with the edge of the platform, you won't be able to install joist hangers properly. Instead, use framing anchors.

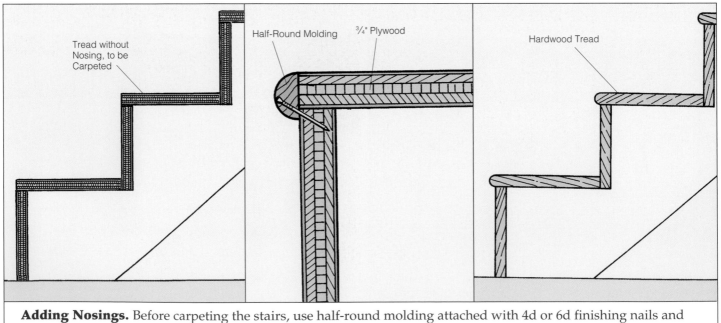

Adding Nosings. Before carpeting the stairs, use half-round molding attached with 4d or 6d finishing nails and construction adhesive to create nosings. Hardwood can be installed so that it overhangs the risers.

other stairs

Ladder Stairs. A ladder-like stairway takes up little floor space.

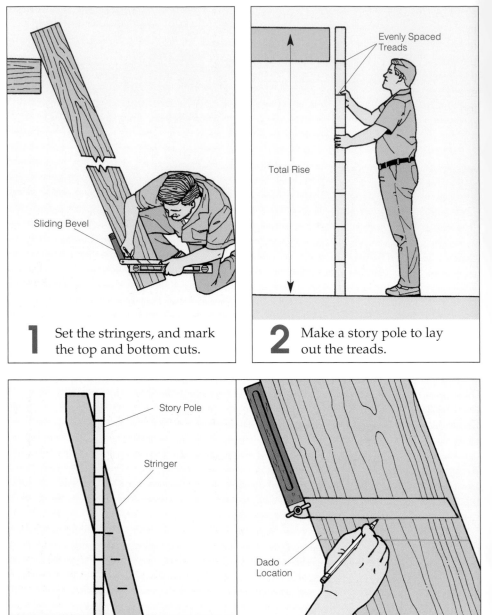

1 Set the stringers, and mark the top and bottom cuts.

2 Make a story pole to lay out the treads.

3 Use the story pole and a sliding bevel to lay out the dado locations on the stringers.

Ladder Stairs

A ladder stairway comes in handy for gaining access to an attic or loft. Because ladder stairs are so steep, codes prohibit the use of ladder stairs in a regularly used or occupied part of the house.

Ladder stairs require little floor space, and the open-riser design won't obstruct the view from one side of the room to the other. You can use dimensional lumber (2x8 stringers and 2x6 treads, for example), 5/4 oak, or another hardwood. The treads rest in dadoes cut in the stringers. Because the ladder stairway has only two stringers, the treads should be kept to 30 inches or less in width.

Because this staircase is neither required nor covered by codes, the rise and run requirements discussed at length on pages 18 to 20 probably won't apply, but check with your building inspector before proceeding. For this kind of stairway, a rise of between 10 and 12 inches is best. Ladder stairs are intended for permanent installation. If you need the access but don't want to tie up floor space, consider installing folding stairs. (See "Folding Attic Stairs," page 50.)

1 **Preparing the Stringers.** Set the stringers in place. The angle at which they will rest depends on your preference. A good target slope is between 60 and 70 degrees. Use a 24-inch level and sliding bevel to establish the cut line on the bottom of each stringer. Make the horizontal cuts; put the stringers back in place; and use the sliding bevel to mark the top horizontal and vertical cuts.

2 **Making the Story Pole.** A story pole is a quick and accurate tool for laying out the stringers. Use a straight board to make the story pole. Set the board in the opening. Use a level to make sure the board is perfectly plumb; then mark the upper floor surface on the story pole. Measure from this mark to the bottom of the pole to determine the total rise. Divide the total rise by the number of treads you desire, and mark the treads on the story pole.

3 **Laying Out the Stringers.** Rest the stringers in place, and holding the story pole plumb, transfer the layout onto the inside face of each stringer. If necessary, use a framing square to extend the layout on the story pole to the stringer. Use the sliding bevel, set to the angle established in Step 1, to mark the layout for the dadoes. Because the story pole is laid out with the tops of the treads, marking the dadoes involves marking more layout lines one tread thickness below the original layout.

4 **Cutting the Dadoes.** The simplest way to cut the dadoes is to use a table saw and dado cutter. You can also make a series of freehand cuts using a circular saw. Set the blade to cut no more than halfway through the board. Cut carefully and stay within the layout lines. Clean out the dadoes using a chisel. If you have a router, you can make clean, accurate dadoes using a straight bit. A simple, temporary fence made of 1x4 stock will help guide the router, as shown.

5 **Assembling the Ladder.** Cut the treads to length; then temporarily assemble the entire ladder on the floor to ensure that the parts fit. Take the ladder apart; apply glue to the dadoes and tread ends; and reassemble it. Use clamps at the upper and lower treads to help hold the ladder square; then drill pilot holes and drive 2 ½-inch wood screws through the stringers into the treads.

6 **Installing the Ladder.** Use metal framing anchors or heavy-duty angle-iron brackets to secure the top of the stringers to the wall or framing. If joists run alongside the outside faces of the stringers, fasten the joists and stringers with two carriage bolts through each side. The bottoms should be toenailed to the floor or secured with brackets.

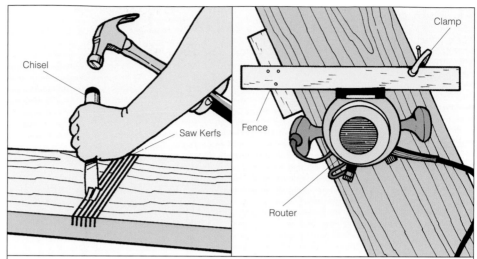

4 Cut the dadoes without a table saw by making a series of kerfs using a circular saw. Chisel out the waste. For greater accuracy, use a router.

5 Assemble the ladder by gluing and screwing the stringers to the treads. Use clamps to hold the assembly square.

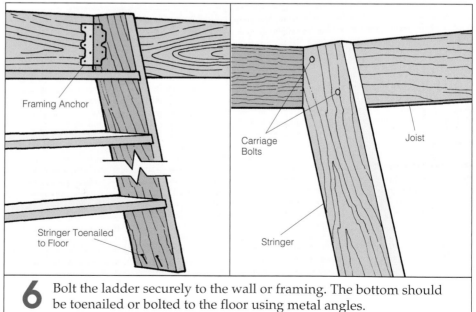

6 Bolt the ladder securely to the wall or framing. The bottom should be toenailed or bolted to the floor using metal angles.

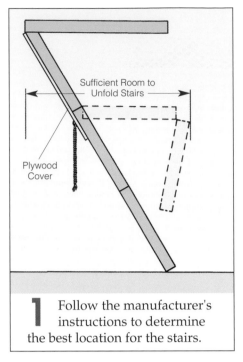

Follow the manufacturer's instructions to determine the best location for the stairs.

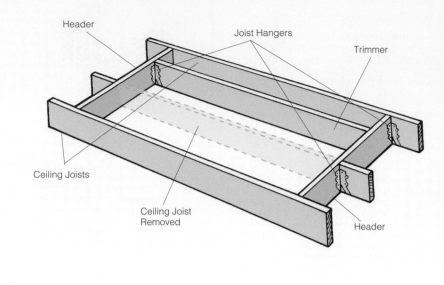

2 Most attic stairs are installed parallel with the ceiling joists. Frame the rough opening by cutting out a section of a joist and installing two headers and one trimmer. Use joist hangers.

Folding Attic Stairs

Folding stairs are intended to provide access to an attic. When you need to get into the attic, you pull down the stairs; when you're done with them, they fold back up into the attic.

Folding stairs are sold as kits at building-supply outlets and are designed to be installed quickly. The instructions that follow are typical of folding-staircase designs, but make sure to follow the manufacturer's specific recommendations.

1 **Locating the Stairs.** The stairs must be located where there is sufficient room to swing the ladder open, and you must have enough floor space around the bottom to allow safe access on and off the ladder. Check the dimensions required for installing folding stairs before you buy them.

2 **Framing the Rough Opening.** Most often, the stairs will be installed so that they run parallel with the ceiling joists. You will have to cut a section out of at least one joist, so install headers and trimmers to create the rough opening. The illustration shows the removal of a section of one joist and the installation of two headers and a trimmer.

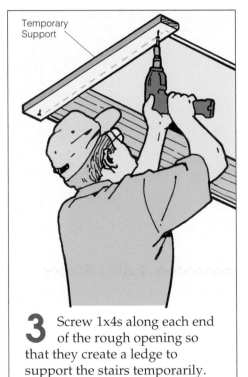

3 Screw 1x4s along each end of the rough opening so that they create a ledge to support the stairs temporarily.

3 **Installing Temporary Supports.** Temporarily screw 1x4 supports across the ends of the rough opening so that they form a 1-inch ledge in the opening. Drive 2-inch drywall screws through the 1x4 supports into the headers on both ends of the rough opening. The supports will be required to carry the full weight of the stairs.

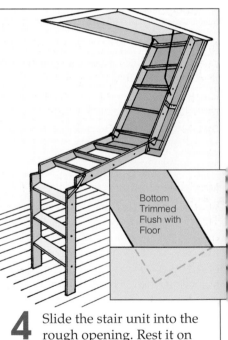

4 Slide the stair unit into the rough opening. Rest it on the 1x4 supports. When the unit is level and square, secure it.

4 **Installing the Stairs.** With a helper in the attic, slide the staircase unit up into the rough opening, and rest it on the temporary supports. Make sure that you've placed it in the right direction. Level and square the frame, using wood shims if necessary. Carefully unfold the stairs, and then drive 10d nails or 2½-inch screws through the stairway

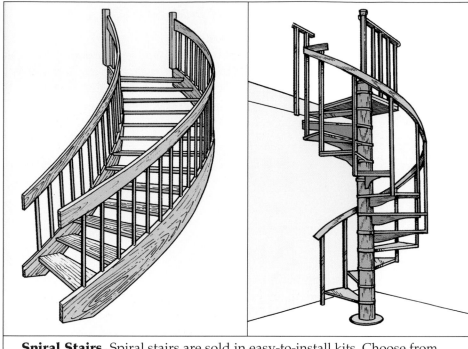

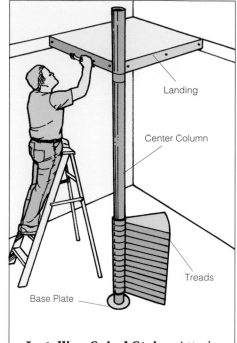

Spiral Stairs. Spiral stairs are sold in easy-to-install kits. Choose from metal or wood, for interior or exterior applications.

Installing Spiral Stairs. Attach the base, landing, and treads.

frame into the joists. Trim the bottom of the stairs flush with the floor so that when unfolded the ladder forms a straight line. Remove the temporary supports, and trim the opening with casing.

Spiral Stairs

Many people find spiral stairs to be an attractive architectural feature. Their main purpose, though, is to allow a transition from one level to the next without consuming a lot of room. A 48-inch-diameter spiral staircase can be tucked into a corner of a room with little or no interruption of household traffic flow, or it can be installed in a more central location in a room without creating a bottleneck.

Spiral stairs don't have to be compact. There are some grand designs that make a gradual, sloping, 90-degree turn. An advantage of this style is that it may be used as a primary stairway. Codes dictate that standard spiral stairs, which make a 270-degree turn, be used only as utility stairs.

Only a skilled craftsperson would want to make a spiral staircase from scratch. Fortunately, there are several manufacturers of spiral stairs for interior and exterior applications. These stairs can be delivered to your home ready for installation. You may be surprised at the variety of styles and materials available. Check with local building-supply outlets and look through home-improvement magazines for the names of spiral-staircase manufacturers.

Installing Spiral Stairs

Installation techniques vary widely, depending on the manufacturer and

the style you choose. The illustrations provide an idea of the components that make up a typical spiral stairway kit. Installation usually begins with the base plate, which is bolted to the floor. A center column is then fastened to the base plate, usually via a threaded rod, and the treads are attached to the column. The top tread attaches to the landing, which is bolted to the stairwell framing.

Platform Stairs

It's not necessary to cut out stringers when you only need a single step. A platform stair is simple to make, yet it

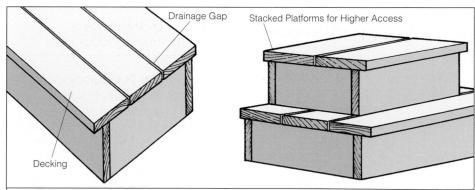

Platform Stairs. Instead of laying out and cutting stringers, build simple platforms for access to a low deck or patio.

1 Rip the boards for the platform frame to size, and then assemble it using 10d nails.

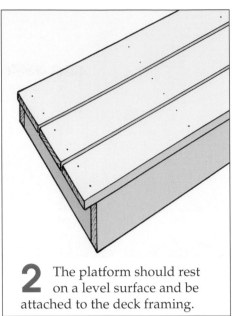

2 The platform should rest on a level surface and be attached to the deck framing.

Dry-Set Brick Step

This exterior stair is a good choice when all you need is a single step up to a deck or gazebo. "Dry-set" bricks do not require any mortar or concrete. Instead, they are set on a bed of compacted gravel topped with a layer of sand. The bricks, sand, and gravel are contained in a frame of pressure-treated or decay-resistant two-by lumber. Instead of bricks, you could also use concrete pavers.

1 **Building the Frame.** Measure the total rise, which is the distance from the ground to the decking surface. Divide this figure in half to determine the riser height.

Rip the frame lumber to the riser height. Cut the front and back risers to the width of the step, then cut ¾-inch by 1½-inch rabbets on each side. Cut the side risers to length, then nail or screw the corners from each direction, as shown.

2 **Assembling the Step.** Prepare a reasonably level surface, then set the frame in place. Lay landscaping fabric in the bottom, then fill the frame with pea gravel, sand, and bricks. Fill any gaps between bricks by sweeping sand over the surface.

---

can match your deck or gazebo nicely if you use decking boards for the treads. You can adjust the unit rise by changing the height of the platform frame. And you can stack one platform on top of another to create multi-riser stairs.

1 **Building the Frame.** Measure the distance from the ground to the decking surface. Divide this figure in half, then subtract the thickness of the tread boards (1½ inches

for 2x4s or 2x6s) to get the height of your platform.

Rip the boards for the platform to size. If you are using pressure-treated lumber, be sure to treat the cut edges with preservative before proceeding. Nail the platform together.

2 **Assembling the Stair.** Prepare a level surface for the stair platform. Fasten the platform to the deck beam or rim joist; then cover the platform with decking boards.

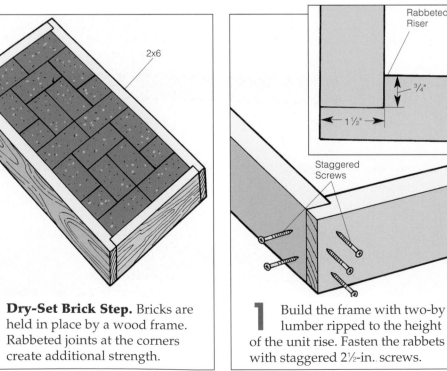

Dry-Set Brick Step. Bricks are held in place by a wood frame. Rabbeted joints at the corners create additional strength.

1 Build the frame with two-by lumber ripped to the height of the unit rise. Fasten the rabbets with staggered 2½-in. screws.

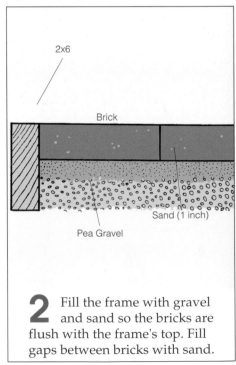

2 Fill the frame with gravel and sand so the bricks are flush with the frame's top. Fill gaps between bricks with sand.

railings

Balustrades

A balustrade can be the most prominent, and therefore aesthetically significant, feature of a staircase. Balustrades also serve an important safety function, providing both a graspable handrail to steady the user and a blockade on open stairs to prevent a fall over the side.

Balustrade Types

There are two principle kinds of balustrades: post-to-post and over-the-post. On a post-to-post railing, the handrail is cut to fit between newel posts, and all of the handrail sections are straight. This design is easier to build than an over-the-post balustrade, which has a continuous handrail that's attached to the tops of the posts. Although many homeowners favor the flowing appearance of an over-the-post balustrade, fabricating one from scratch is difficult even for experienced stair builders. If your heart is set on an over-the-post balustrade, consider installing a prefabricated

system. On the other hand, you can build an attractive post-to-post balustrade yourself using a table saw and router. Prefabricated components are also available. Check building-supply outlets for their stock on hand, or ask to see catalogs from manufacturers of stairway and stair parts. This chapter will give you basic design choices and construction techniques for both styles of balustrade, with emphasis on post-to-post balustrades.

Building a Balustrade

Building your own balustrade can be as easy or difficult as you want to make it. A post-to-post design with doweled balusters set in the treads and fillets at the handrail can take a good deal of time, whereas a design with balusters nailed to the sides of a stringer can be finished in very little time. The type of balustrade you build will depend on the location of the stairs (inside vs. outside, basement vs. main floor), your time and confidence, and your budget.

Establishing the Balustrade Centerline. If you want to build a balustrade system with balusters set in the treads, you first must establish the balustrade centerline. This is nothing more than a common point along which all of the components can be located.

There are no hard-and-fast rules about where exactly to locate the balustrade centerline, but there are a few general rules of thumb, which you can follow to the letter or deviate from as necessary. A good method for establishing the centerline is to begin with the location of the balusters on the treads. Balusters typically align on the side with the face of the stringer or skirtboard. Thus, the balustrade centerline is located exactly half the width of a baluster away from the face of the stringer or skirtboard. Mark the centerline in pencil on each tread.

Remember that codes usually require at least 32 inches of clearance at the handrail on a 36-inch-wide staircase. Be sure to check the

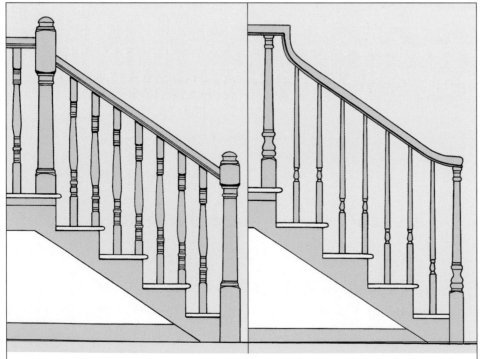

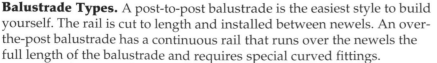

Balustrade Types. A post-to-post balustrade is the easiest style to build yourself. The rail is cut to length and installed between newels. An over-the-post balustrade has a continuous rail that runs over the newels the full length of the balustrade and requires special curved fittings.

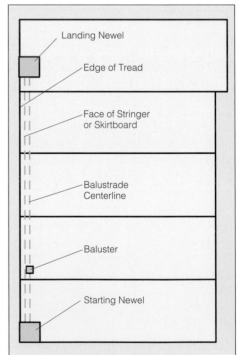

Establishing the Balustrade Centerline. The balustrade centerline locates the midpoint of the railing.

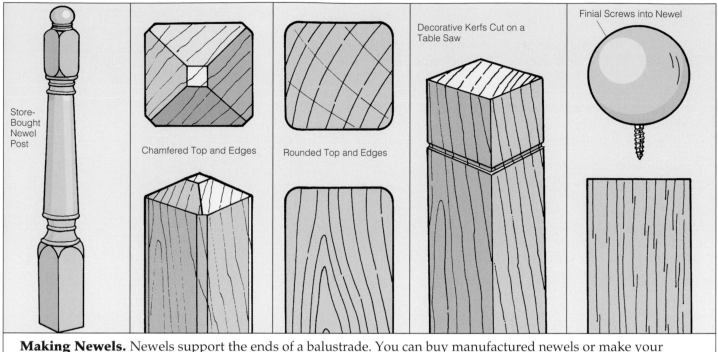

Making Newels. Newels support the ends of a balustrade. You can buy manufactured newels or make your own from 4x4 lumber. Simple decorative touches, such as cutting chamfers and kerfs or attaching finials, will add to the beauty of custom-built newels.

requirements in your area. Check the clearance after you establish the centerline, keeping in mind that half the width of the handrail extends beyond the centerline.

Making Newels

Newels, or newel posts, are the backbone of the balustrade system, making it strong and reliable. As a general rule, you need one newel at the bottom of the stairs, one at the top, and one at a landing or any other change of direction. The newel at the bottom of the stairs is called the starting newel; the landing newel is at the top. An L-shaped staircase that is open along one side also needs an angle or platform newel (or newels) to allow the railing to turn the corner. An angle newel requires complex notching, work that is probably best left to a professional. (See the sidebar "Turning Corners," page 56, for more information.)

You can make your own newel posts if you want a simple, straightforward design. For a more complex profile, you might want to shop for a manufactured newel. If you choose to

make your own, use good-quality 4x4 lumber. If you're making a hardwood newel post but can't find large enough stock, you'll have to glue up two smaller pieces. Chamfer or round over the edges of the 4x4. You can add a decorative touch to the top of the post with a manufactured finial, which can be screwed onto the post. You can also create a band of decorative kerfs around the post using a table saw or a router.

Installing Newels

With the balustrade centerline determined, you can calculate where to locate the newels. The aim is to center each newel on the centerline. With the handrail centered over the balusters, this ensures that the handrail will fall in the center of the newel.

1 **Laying Out the Newels.** Use the centerline to determine where to notch the newel. Some

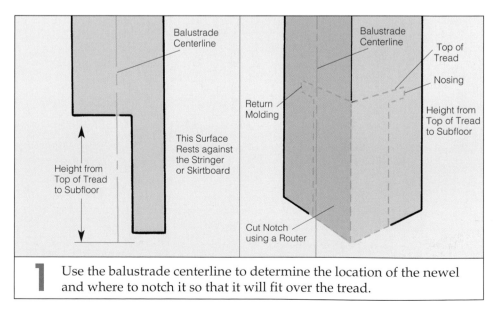

1 Use the balustrade centerline to determine the location of the newel and where to notch it so that it will fit over the tread.

newels require a notch on one face only; others must fit around the corner of a tread. The illustrations give general guidelines for calculating the notch on a newel that rests on the subfloor. If the newel is going to be attached to the framing beneath the subfloor, you will need to adjust the length accordingly.

2 **Cutting the Notches.** You can cut a simple side notch using a circular saw and chisel. With the depth of the saw blade set to the depth of the notch, make a series of cuts. Then clean out the notch using a chisel.

A corner notch should be cut using a router fitted with a straight bit. You need to rout on two sides, then clean out the corners using a chisel. If the

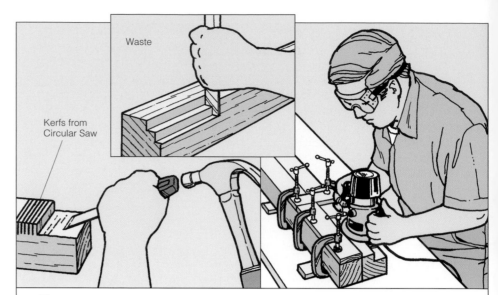

2 Use a circular saw and chisel to cut a side notch in the newel (left). To cut a corner notch, use a router with a straight bit to clamp straight boards to the 4x4 to guide the router (right). Square the corners and remove waste using a hammer and chisel (inset).

Turning Corners

A handrail on an L-shaped stairway can be short and simple or complex, depending on whether the staircase is open or enclosed by walls. If the entire stairway is enclosed by walls on both sides, you need only add a basic wall rail. If the bottom run is open (left), you can install a straight handrail following the instructions in this chapter.

If one entire side of the stairs is open, however, you will have to install a handrail around the corner. One approach is to use a double newel post (middle), essentially two separate, straight handrails. This utilitarian approach is best suited to basement stairs.

The most attractive—and complex—way to turn the corner is by using an

angle newel (right). Notching angle newels is difficult work that you might want to leave to a trained stair builder. When notched correctly, an angle newel laps the skirtboard on both the lower and upper staircase runs. Because the bottom of the newel is visible at the corner of the finished wall, it often is chamfered for a decorative touch.

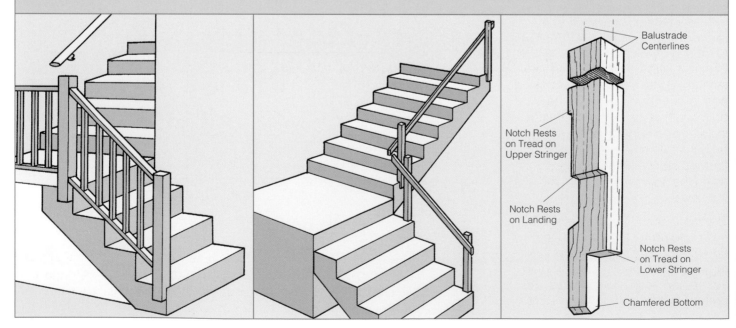

The newel must be strong and fastened securely. Whenever possible, make the post is long enough to extend through the subfloor; bolt it to the floor joists or blocking between the joists. If the floors, walls, and ceilings have already been finished, this effort may be too involved. But if you can cut out a section of the subflooring and get at the framing beneath without much effort, you can create a stronger connection for the newel post.

The newel may need to be notched to fit over a floor joist. Attach the newel to the joist with two carriage bolts (left). If the newel falls between two floor joists, add cross blocking and bolt the newel to the blocking (middle). Another option is to install a base for the newel by nailing a piece of two-by lumber to the bottoms of the joists and securing the newel with lag screws (right).

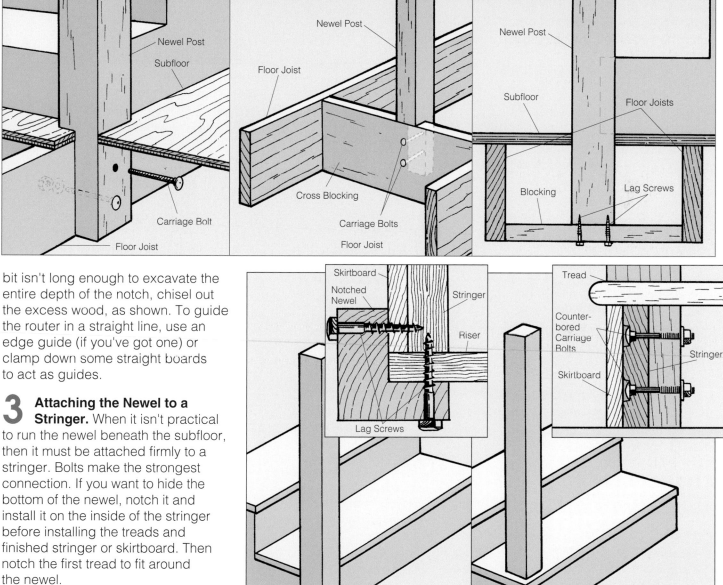

bit isn't long enough to excavate the entire depth of the notch, chisel out the excess wood, as shown. To guide the router in a straight line, use an edge guide (if you've got one) or clamp down some straight boards to act as guides.

3 **Attaching the Newel to a Stringer.** When it isn't practical to run the newel beneath the subfloor, then it must be attached firmly to a stringer. Bolts make the strongest connection. If you want to hide the bottom of the newel, notch it and install it on the inside of the stringer before installing the treads and finished stringer or skirtboard. Then notch the first tread to fit around the newel.

The more common approach is to notch the newel to fit around the corner of the bottom tread, which may have to be notched as well to accept the newel. In this case, the bottom of the newel will be visible.

3 If it's too difficult to attach the newel to the floor framing, bolt it to a stringer. Notch the newel to fit over the outside of the stringer and tread (left) or over the inside of the stringer (right).

Carriage bolts or lag screws can be driven through the post on two sides. Check the newel post for plumb on two adjacent sides before tightening the bolts. Countersink the holes, if you like, and then cover the bolt heads with wood plugs.

Handrails

Manufactured Handrails

Handrails come in a variety of shapes and sizes. You can buy a manufactured handrail and cut it to length or make your own, but remember that the handrail serves one principal function: It gives you something to grab onto when climbing or descending the stairs. If the handrail can't be gripped, it can't do its job. That is why codes give specific instructions on the size and shape of the handrail. A round handrail with a diameter between 1¼ and 2 inches is the most effective size for grasping purposes. Most building-supply outlets carry several styles of handrails manufactured to meet code requirements.

Making a Handrail

If you are making the newels and balusters yourself, you may want to make a matching handrail. The handrail at left in the illustration can be made using a solid piece of wood or with two ⁵⁄₄ (1-inch-thick) boards glued together. You'll need a router table to plow out the groove on the bottom, cut the coves along the sides for gripping purposes, and round over the top edges.

A simple handrail that's ideal for stairs to a deck or basement is the T-shaped design. It has a graspable 2-inch-wide board on top that is 1 inch to 1½ inches thick, and nailed or screwed to a vertical 2x6. The 2x6 can be attached to newel posts. A variation of this design uses only a 2x6 with finger grips routed out.

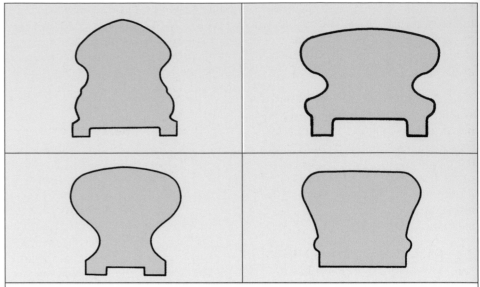

Manufactured Handrails. Prefabricated handrails come in a wide variety of styles. They can be purchased with a flat or a dadoed (plowed) bottom. Choose one that matches your overall balustrade design and installation technique.

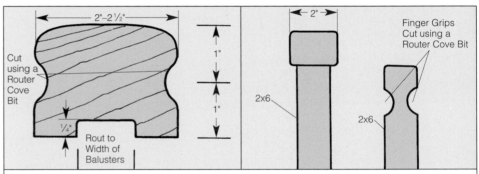

Making a Handrail. If you want to make your own handrail, be sure that it can be grasped securely. If it can't, it isn't safe. Although you can use a router to shape a handrail, it can be as simple as a pair of boards nailed together to form a "T" shape.

Installing a Handrail

For this post-to-post balustrade, the handrail fits between newel posts with a butt joint cut at the angle of the slope of the stairs. The handrail is attached to the newels with screws or rail bolts. The height at which the rail is fastened depends on local codes, usually between 30 and 38 inches above the tread nosing.

1 Establishing the Angle Cut. First, determine the angle to cut the ends of the handrail. Set a straight board or 48-inch level on the tread nosings so that it crosses the starting newel post. Set a sliding

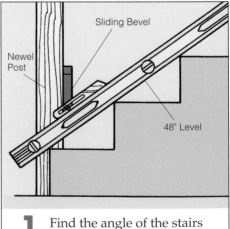

1 Find the angle of the stairs by resting a level across the treads. Transfer the angle to the miter box using a sliding bevel.

bevel to the angle formed between the level and the newel post. Transfer the setting on the sliding bevel to a miter box, chop saw, or table saw, and then make the bottom cut.

2 Cutting Handrails to Length. Lay the rail along the tread nosings flush with the starting newel. Scribe the length of the handrail at the upper newel, then cut. Bear in mind that this method will work only if both newel posts are plumb. If they aren't, you should cut the handrail a little long, then trim it for a good fit.

3 Establishing Handrail Height. The height of the handrail is established by codes and is measured vertically from the nosing of the treads. Usually, the minimum is 30 inches and the maximum is 38 inches. Clamp a piece of wood on the newel post to hold the handrail at the appropriate height.

4 Fastening Handrails to Newels. There are several ways to attach the handrail to the newel post. The method you use may be dictated by the style of the handrail. If you are using a handrail with a grooved, or plowed, bottom, you can drive two 2-inch drywall screws through the underside of the handrail into the starting newel post at the base of the stairs. Later, the balusters and fillets will cover the screw holes.

Another method uses rail bolts. A rail bolt has machine-screw threads on one end and lag-screw threads on the other. With the handrail temporarily clamped in place, counterbore a large-diameter access hole about 1 ½ inches deep for the washer and nut. Then drill a pilot hole through the handrail 2 inches deep into the newel post for the bolt itself. Remove the handrail and screw the lag-screw end of the rail bolt into the newel post. This will be easier if you spin a couple of nuts on the machine thread end, then use a wrench to

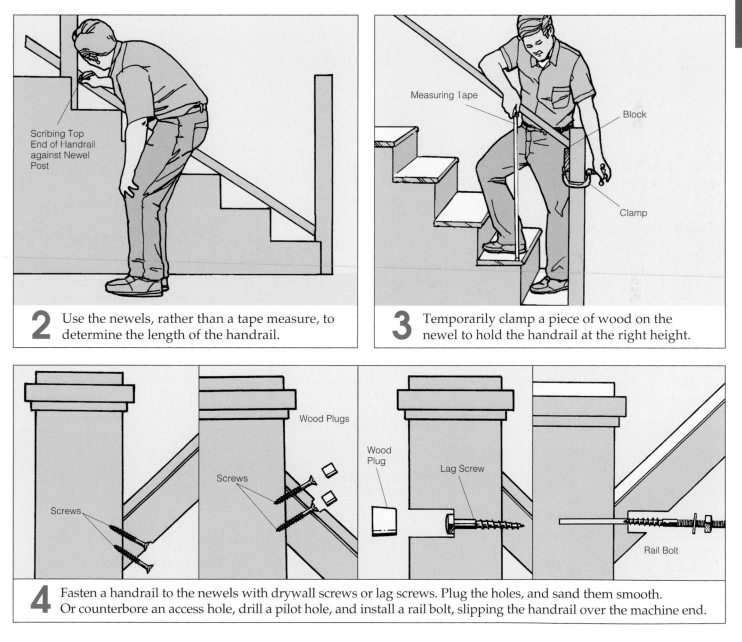

Scribing Top End of Handrail against Newel Post

2 Use the newels, rather than a tape measure, to determine the length of the handrail.

Measuring Tape

Block

Clamp

3 Temporarily clamp a piece of wood on the newel to hold the handrail at the right height.

Wood Plugs

Screws

Screws

Wood Plug

Lag Screw

Rail Bolt

4 Fasten a handrail to the newels with drywall screws or lag screws. Plug the holes, and sand them smooth. Or counterbore an access hole, drill a pilot hole, and install a rail bolt, slipping the handrail over the machine end.

grip the nuts and thread the bolt in. Slip the handrail over the rail bolt, insert the washer; then tighten the nut. The access hole can be covered with a wood plug.

The top end of the handrail should be attached with screws through the bottom or with screws or a lag screw through the top. Plug the holes.

Installing Wall Rails

In an enclosed stairwell where there are walls on both sides of the stairs, you need only attach a rail to the wall. The height of the wall rail is established by code, usually between 30 and 38 inches. Also, you must maintain a space of at least 1 ½ inches between the handrail and the wall.

The easiest method for installing a wall rail is to attach a stock handrail to brackets that are fastened to the wall. The brackets must be secured with screws long enough to penetrate at least halfway into the wall studs or blocking. With the brackets in place, cut the handrail to length and attach it to the brackets with screws.

Making a Wall Rail. If you're not satisfied with the look of a manufactured wall rail, you can make your own. Use a router to round the top and shape the finger grips on a 2x4. Use 1 ½-inch spacers, such as wood dowels, to hold the handrail away from the wall, and drive lag screws through the handrail into the wall framing. Cover the lag-screw holes with wood plugs, if desired.

Building Basic Railings

If you need a railing on your basement, deck, or porch stairs, or if you just prefer a simpler design, you can build a more basic model that doesn't require fitting balusters into treads and handrails. With this basic railing, the posts are notched and then bolted to the staircase stringer. A top and bottom rail are nailed to the posts, with balusters then nailed

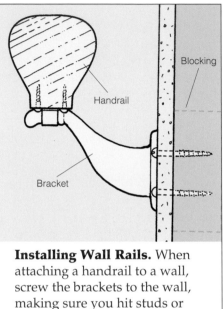

Installing Wall Rails. When attaching a handrail to a wall, screw the brackets to the wall, making sure you hit studs or blocking, and then screw the handrail to the brackets.

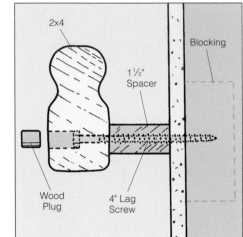

Making a Wall Rail. Use a router to shape a 2x4 into a custom-made wall rail. Use dowels to hold the rail away from the wall, or cut 1 ½-in. lengths of metal tubing.

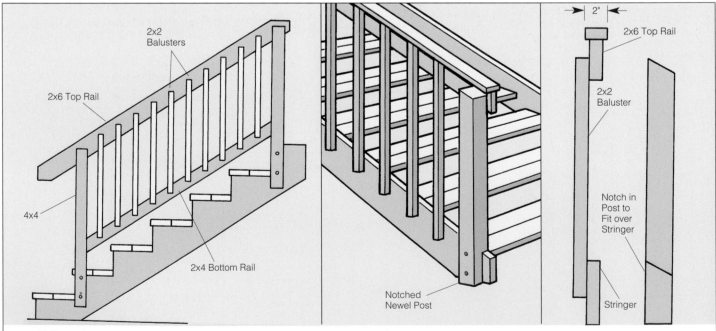

Building Basic Railings. Functional and attractive railings can be made using simple techniques and basic materials. The one- and two-rail designs shown are ideal for exterior and basement stairs.

to the rails. A variation on this design eliminates the bottom rail, with the bottoms of the balusters secured to the face of the stringer.

As a handrail, a 2x6 top rail set on edge may suffice for a short run of stairs, but a more graspable handrail can be formed by nailing a 2-inch-wide cap rail on top of the top rail.

1 Notching the Posts. To notch a post, set the blade on your circular saw to the depth of the notch. (1½ inches will give the post full bearing on the stringer.) Make a series of cuts through the post, then clean out the notch using a chisel.

2 Installing the Posts. To fasten a post on a stringer, have a

helper hold the post plumb using a level. Drill pilot holes through the post and stringer. Insert ⅜-inch carriage bolts, washers, and nuts, then tighten securely.

3 Installing Rails and Balusters. With 10d common nails, nail the rail or rails to the post; then use 8d finishing nails to attach the 2x2 balusters to the rails. To keep the balusters equally spaced and plumb, you may want to make a baluster-spacing template. For a 4-inch gap, nail a 4-inch-wide spacer board to a short 2x4. The 2x4 should be at the slope of the top rail, while the spacer should be plumb. You can establish this angle quickly by laying the 2x4 along the top rail and the spacer against the newel post, then nailing them together.

Balusters

Balusters, sometimes called spindles, aren't just pretty to look at; they also support the handrail and fill the gap between the handrail and treads. Building codes regulate the size of gap that is permitted between balusters, normally 4 to 6 inches. This tight spacing not only prevents a child from falling through the balustrade, it

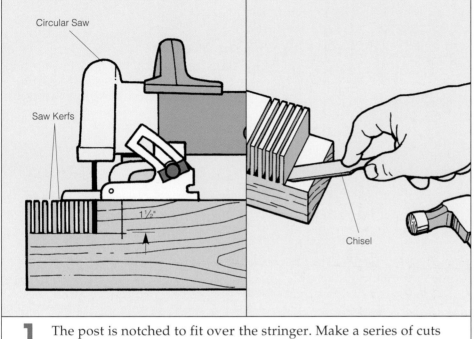

1 The post is notched to fit over the stringer. Make a series of cuts to the proper depth using a circular saw, then clean out the waste using a chisel.

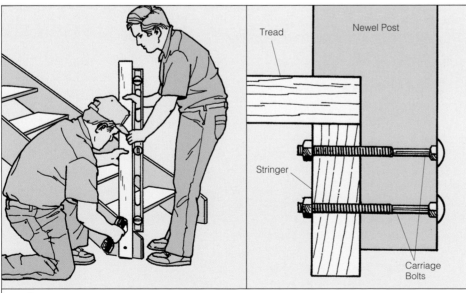

2 Have a helper hold the newel post plumb while you drill pilot holes through the post and stringer. Secure the post to the stringer with 4-in.-long, ⅜-in.-diameter carriage bolts.

3 Nail balusters to rails with 8d finishing nails. For even spacing, make a template.

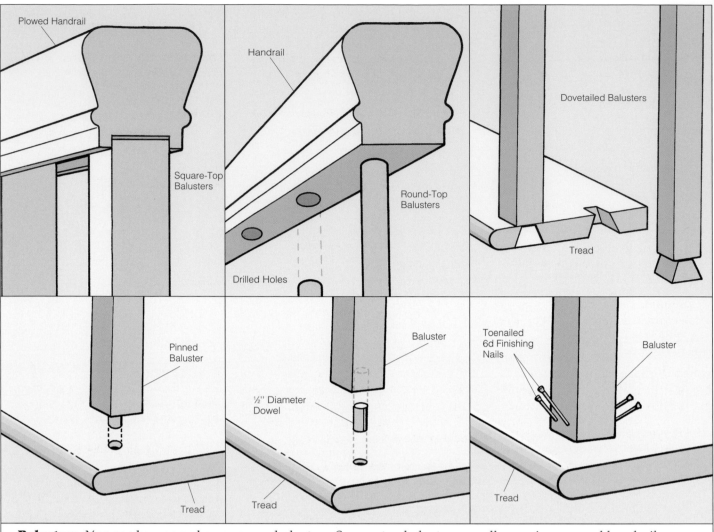

Balusters. You can buy or make your own balusters. Square-top balusters usually require grooved handrails, while rounded balusters are set in holes in the handrail. Manufactured balusters have pins that fit into holes in the stair treads; homemade balusters may be doweled or nailed to treads. Space balusters 4 to 6 inches apart, with the shorter baluster installed at the front of the tread and the longer in back.

is also intended to prevent small children from slipping their heads between balusters. A 4-inch gap is much more effective in this regard.

Balusters usually are designed to mimic the style of the newel posts, but they don't have to be. Rounded balusters, for example, can offer a pleasant contrast to bulky, square newels. If you'd like to make your own rounded balusters, they can be fashioned out of large-diameter hardwood dowels or closet poles, both of which are available at building-supply outlets. Simple square balusters can be fashioned from hardwood stock and cut to size on your table saw.

At one time, experienced stair-builders attached balusters to treads with dovetail joints, but such labor-intensive joinery is rarely seen in new construction. Today, manufactured balusters are available with wood pins on the base that fit into holes bored in the treads. Balusters that you make yourself can be toenailed to the treads or set with dowels. The tops of balusters are either rounded or square. Square-top balusters usually are installed in the groove of a plowed handrail; if you make your own square balusters, cut them just wide enough to fit the groove. Rounded balusters are set in holes drilled in the underside of the handrail.

For balusters that are attached between treads and the handrail, note that you will need two sizes. The baluster at the front of the tread is shorter than the back baluster. Also note that the lines of any recess or chamfer on the baluster are horizontal to the tread at the bottom but follow the slope of the handrail at the top.

Installing Balusters

Whether you buy them pre-milled or make your own, the easiest way to install balusters is to set them in holes drilled in the treads. The holes are drilled along the balustrade centerline, and they accept the pins in the bottoms of manufactured bal-

If you arbitrarily space balusters a certain distance apart, say 4 inches, the space between the last baluster and the newel post may not be the same as the rest of the spaces. To ensure equal spacing between all balusters, you'll have to do some math.

1. Add the width of one baluster to the targeted spacing between balusters (1.5 + 4 = 5.5).

2. Divide the vertical spacing between posts by the result in #1 (84.5 ÷ 5.5 = 15.36).

3. Round the result in #2 down to determine the number of balusters needed (15).

4. Multiply the number of balusters by the width of one baluster (15 x 1.5 = 22.5).

5. Subtract the result in #4 from the spacing between the posts (84.5 - 22.5 = 62).

6. Add 1 to the number of balusters to account for the extra space that occurs in a balustrade (15 + 1 = 16).

7. Divide the result in #5 by the result in #6 (62 ÷ 16 = 3.875).

8. Convert the result in #7 into a fractional equivalent for the spacing between each baluster, and make space to this size (3.875 = 3⅞).

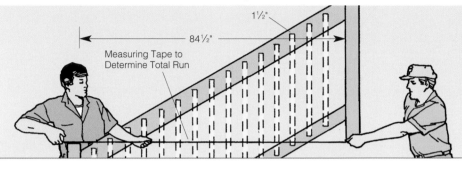

1½"

84½"

Measuring Tape to Determine Total Run

---

usters. If you're making your own balusters, you should insert dowels in the ends.

1 Laying Out the Treads. Having established the balustrade centerline, you've already done most of the work for laying out the baluster locations on the treads. On a typical balustrade, each tread holds two balusters. The face of the front baluster aligns with the face of the riser beneath it. The back baluster is

centered between the risers. This layout procedure will ensure that the balusters are equally spaced. Make sure that the spacing between balusters meets your local code.

2 Boring the Treads. If you're installing pre-milled balusters with bottom pins, or if you plan to use dowels to fasten custom-made balusters to the treads, you must drill holes in the treads. Draw straight diagonal lines in each baluster out-

line, and at the intersection of the lines, drill a hole 1 inch deep using a brad-point bit of the appropriate diameter. Drill straight holes.

3 Cutting Balusters to Length. The length of each baluster should be measured in place. That way you will be assured of a tight fit at each joint. Hold the baluster in place, using a level to keep it perfectly plumb. Scribe a line across the baluster where it intersects the bottom of the handrail.

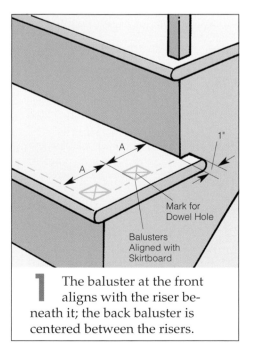

Mark for Dowel Hole

Balusters Aligned with Skirtboard

1 The baluster at the front aligns with the riser beneath it; the back baluster is centered between the risers.

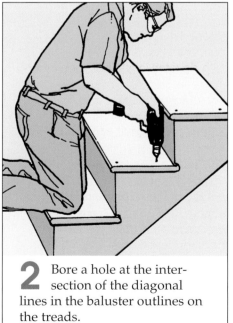

2 Bore a hole at the intersection of the diagonal lines in the baluster outlines on the treads.

3 Hold each baluster over its layout mark; use a level to check it for plumb; then mark the top for cutting.

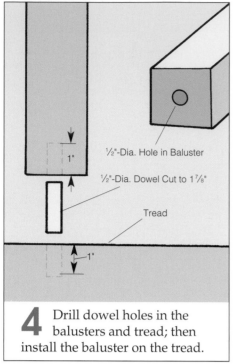

½"-Dia. Hole in Baluster

½"-Dia. Dowel Cut to 1⅞"

1"

Tread

1"

4 Drill dowel holes in the balusters and tread; then install the baluster on the tread.

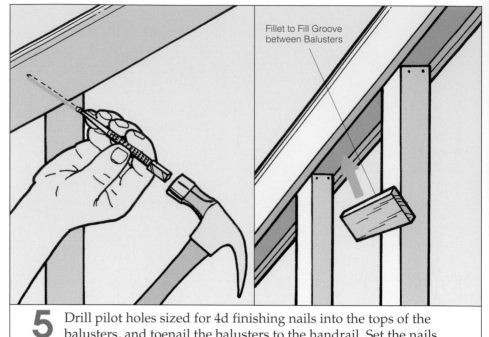

Fillet to Fill Groove between Balusters

5 Drill pilot holes sized for 4d finishing nails into the tops of the balusters, and toenail the balusters to the handrail. Set the nails on a flat-bottomed handrail, or install fillets on a plowed handrail.

Then add to this length the depth of the groove on the handrail.

4 **Doweling Custom-Made Balusters.** Most manufactured balusters come with a 1-inch pin milled on the bottom. You can make a similar detail on your own balusters using ½-inch-diameter dowels. Find the center of the baluster by drawing diagonal lines across the bottom. To drill a perfectly straight hole, you'll have to set up the baluster in a drill press. If you're using a hand drill, secure the baluster in a vise. Drill the hole 1 inch deep. Cut the dowels about ⅛ inch shorter than 2 inches; spread a small amount of glue in the holes and on the dowel; insert the dowel in the baluster, and then install the baluster and dowel on the tread.

5 **Fastening the Baluster Tops.** Toenail the tops of the balusters to the handrail through pilot holes. If the handrail isn't grooved, you will want to set the nails and fill the holes with putty.

On a grooved handrail, the space between balusters is filled with short pieces of wood called fillets. Handrail manufacturers make fillet stock to fit

the groove in a plowed handrail, or you can make your own to match the wood on the handrail and balusters. Establish the angled end cuts of the fillets with a sliding bevel; cut them with a chop saw; and fasten them between balusters with short finishing nails driven into the handrail.

Installing Round-Top Balusters

Any baluster with rounded ends for fitting is a round-top baluster. If

you're installing round-top balusters, you will have to follow a different order of tasks. The handrail should be cut to length, but you won't install it until after the balusters have been fastened to the treads. First, you must drill holes in the underside of the handrail for the balusters. This task will be much easier if you make a pitch block to guide your drill.

1 **Making a Pitch Block.** A pitch block is a triangular piece of wood that is cut to represent the rise,

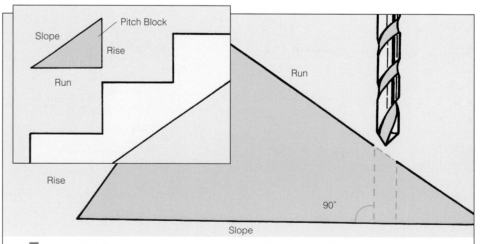

Pitch Block

Slope

Rise

Run

Run

Rise

Slope

90°

1 A pitch block is a triangular piece of wood with sides equal to the rise, run, and slope of the stairs. Drill a hole perpendicular to the slope side and use it to guide your drill when boring the underside of the handrail.

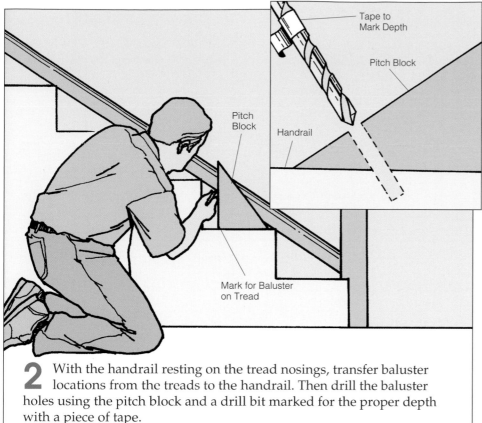

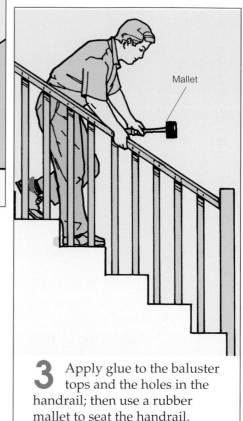

2 With the handrail resting on the tread nosings, transfer baluster locations from the treads to the handrail. Then drill the baluster holes using the pitch block and a drill bit marked for the proper depth with a piece of tape.

3 Apply glue to the baluster tops and the holes in the handrail; then use a rubber mallet to seat the handrail.

run, and slope of the stairs. You can use one of the pieces that were cut out of the stringer, or you can make a new one out of some two-by lumber. Drill a hole perpendicular to the slope side of the block. This hole must be accurate and is best drilled on a drill press with the slope side flat on the table. The drill bit should be the exact diameter of the tops of the balusters. This hole will be your guide for drilling the handrail.

2 Laying Out the Handrail. Cut the handrail to length; then set the handrail along the tread nosings, resting it against the newel posts. Use the pitch block or a framing square to transfer the baluster holes on the treads to the handrail. Drill the holes for the tops of the balusters. To keep the depth of the holes uniform, mark your drill bit with a piece of tape.

3 Installing the Handrail. Temporarily nail or clamp the handrail at its proper height; then cut the balusters to length. Be sure to make the balusters long enough

to fit into the handrail holes. Set all of the balusters in the treads, first spreading glue on the mating surfaces. Align the faces, if necessary. Apply glue to the baluster tops and handrail holes; then install the handrail by tapping it with a rubber mallet.

A helper or two will be useful in fitting the balusters into the handrail holes.

Assembling an Over-the-Post Balustrade

An over-the-post balustrade features a handrail that is mounted on top

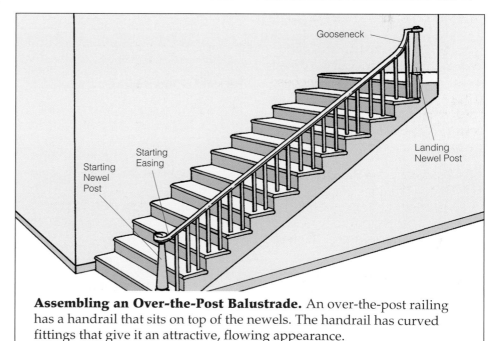

Assembling an Over-the-Post Balustrade. An over-the-post railing has a handrail that sits on top of the newels. The handrail has curved fittings that give it an attractive, flowing appearance.

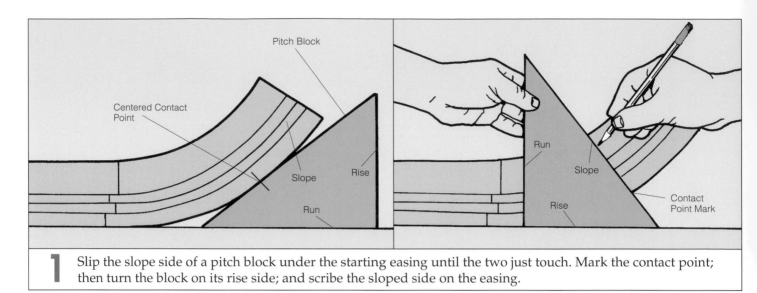

1 Slip the slope side of a pitch block under the starting easing until the two just touch. Mark the contact point; then turn the block on its rise side; and scribe the sloped side on the easing.

of the newel posts. The curved portions of an over-the-post balustrade are called fittings, and they give the railing its flowing appearance. Although it's possible to make your own fittings, manufactured ones are quite attractive and will save you lots of time. This semi-closed, straight-run staircase has two fittings, a starting easing at the bottom and a gooseneck at the top. Use these basic procedures along with manufacturer's instructions to install a manufactured over-the-post handrail.

With an over-the-post balustrade, you assemble the handrail first and then install the newels. To assemble the handrail accurately, you must establish the positions of the newels. In this case, they're notched to fit over the first tread and the top tread, along the centerline of the handrail and the balusters. Some starting newels are offset in a semicircular, or bullnose, starting step, and a curved section of handrail, either a volute or a turnout, connects to the straight part of the handrail. If you're installing a starting step with a volute or turnout, refer to the manufacturer's paper template to lay out the position of the starting newel on the starting step.

1 **Cutting the Starting Easing.**
The first thing to do is to cut the starting easing, which curves upward to join the straight part of the handrail. Set the starting easing on a flat

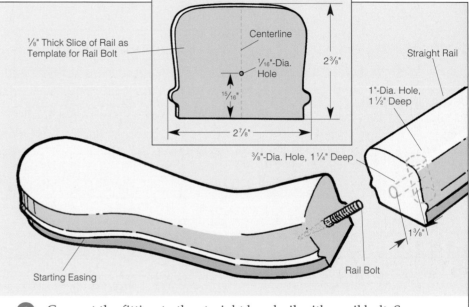

2 Connect the fitting to the straight handrail with a rail bolt. Screw one end into the fitting, and insert the other end into the ⅜-inch hole in the end of the rail. Tighten the nut through the access hole.

surface, then slip a pitch block with the run side down under the curved end of the easing until the sloped side of the block just touches the fitting. Mark this spot on the fitting; then set the pitch block on its rise side so that the sloped side aligns with the pencil mark, and scribe a line. Cut along this line using a chop saw.

2 **Joining the Starting Easing to the Handrail.** Next, square-cut the end of a length of handrail, and join the starting easing to the handrail. Most of the time this connection

is made with a rail bolt. To align the holes for the bolt, make a template. Cut a sliver of handrail from the straight rail, and mark a line down the center. Measure up from the bottom ¹⁵⁄₁₆ inch, and drill a small hole, about ¹⁄₁₆ inch, at the mark. Hold the template on the end of each adjoining rail, and mark the hole. Then bore the pieces for the rail bolt, as shown.

3 **Cutting the Gooseneck Fitting.**
The gooseneck is curved to level off the handrail at the top of the stairs.

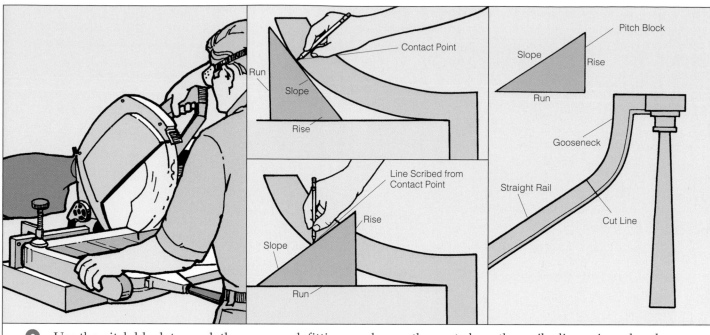

3 Use the pitch block to mark the gooseneck fitting, as shown; then cut along the scribe line using a handsaw or power miter saw.

Set the gooseneck on a flat surface so that the curved end points up, set the pitch block on its rise edge, and slip it under the curve until they're touching. Mark the contact point, flip the pitch block on its run edge, and scribe the angle on the side of the gooseneck. Use a handsaw or chop saw to cut along this line.

4 **Joining the Gooseneck to the Straight Rail.** First rest the assembled portion of the handrail on the steps with the starting easing cap positioned directly over the starting-newel centerpoint. Align the goose-neck cap with the centerpoint of the upstairs newel, making sure the cap is level. Mark the end of the goose-neck on the straight rail, and cut the rail. Install a rail bolt, and fasten the gooseneck to the straight rail. You now have a fully assembled handrail.

5 **Cutting and Installing the Newels.** Set the assembled handrail on the steps, align the caps over the newel centerpoints, and measure the distance between the underside of the starting easing and the first tread or the floor, depending on where the starting newel will sit. To this measurement add the handrail

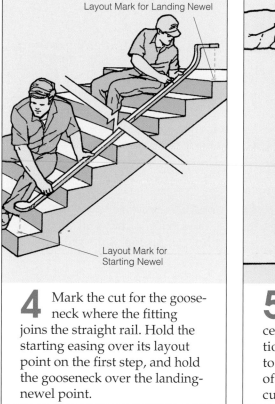

4 Mark the cut for the goose-neck where the fitting joins the straight rail. Hold the starting easing over its layout point on the first step, and hold the gooseneck over the landing-newel point.

height (usually between 30 inches and 38 inches, minus the rail depth because you're measuring to the underside of the rail) to figure out the length of the newel posts. Cut the base of each newel; notch

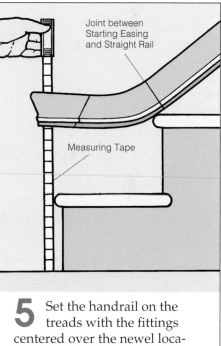

5 Set the handrail on the treads with the fittings centered over the newel loca-tions. Measure from the floor to the handrail; add the height of the installed balusters; and cut the newels to this length.

as necessary; and bolt it to the staircase frame.

6 **Checking the Fit of the Handrail.** Set the handrail so that it locks onto the pins at the tops of the newel posts. If the pins don't fit, use a rasp to file them thinner. With the rail in place, check that the newels are still plumb and that the fittings sit squarely on the newels. Then remove the handrail and make small pencil marks across the joints, as shown. Take the rail apart; glue the joints; and reassemble it, using the pencil marks to realign the joints. Plug all of the holes you made for the rail bolts; plane the plugs flush to the rail surface; and sand them smooth.

7 Marking the Baluster Layout. Scribe a line on the underside of the handrail to indicate the centerline of the handrail. Reset the handrail, and mark it for balusters. Usually their on-center spacing is equal to one-half the tread depth, with two balusters per tread: one even with the face of the riser, the other half a tread-depth away. Mark the baluster centerpoints on the treads; then use a 48-inch level to transfer the layout to the underside of the handrail. Use the pitch block as a template to drill holes for the baluster tops along the centerline of the handrail, as described on pages 64 and 65. If the balusters have pins at their bases, drill holes for them in the treads.

8 Installing the Handrail. Cut the balusters to length; spread a little construction adhesive in the holes; and set the balusters on the treads. Then place the handrail on top of the balusters and newels, and tap it down using a rubber mallet. When you're sure the handrail is seated properly, adjust the balusters so that they're all rotated in the same direction, drill a small pilot hole in the top and bottom of each baluster, and use 4d finishing nails to toenail the balusters to the handrail and treads.

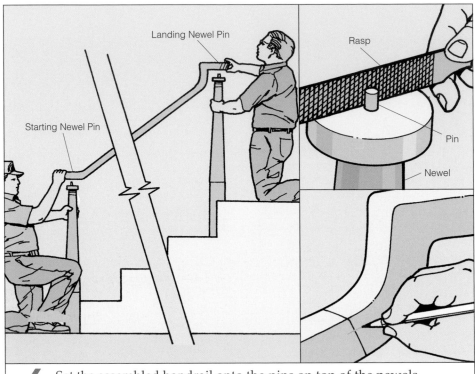

6 Set the assembled handrail onto the pins on top of the newels. Make sure that the rail fits tightly against both newel tops and that the newels are plumb. Then mark the joints as shown, disassemble the handrail, glue it up, and reassemble it.

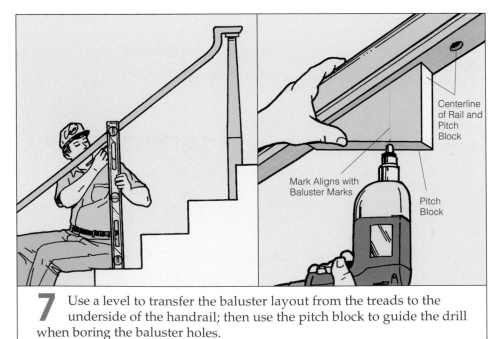

7 Use a level to transfer the baluster layout from the treads to the underside of the handrail; then use the pitch block to guide the drill when boring the baluster holes.

8 Have a helper guide the balusters into the holes as you set the handrail into place.

chapter 8

making repairs

Squeaks

Squeaking stairs are most often caused by wood rubbing against wood or nails. Squeaks develop when the wood shrinks or when fitted parts begin pulling apart. Squeaks can even occur on brand new stairs that were hastily constructed, with less than tight joints between risers, treads, and skirtboard.

Silencing Squeaks from Below

The way to diagnose and repair a squeak is to get under the staircase. Then have a helper upstairs step around the offending spot until you pinpoint the source of the problem. You may want to apply more than one of the following repairs just to be safe.

Shimming the Gaps. If you find any gaps where wood meets wood, force some wood shims into them. Have your helper move around the step to see if the squeak is eliminated. If it is, pull out the shims, coat them with construction adhesive or glue, and replace them.

Replacing Angle Blocks. If your stairs have triangular blocks attached to the tread-riser joint on the underside of each stair, see if they are loose by giving each angle block a light tap with a hammer. If any are loose, remove them, and use sandpaper or a sharp chisel to take off the dried glue. Then replace the angle blocks using screws and construction adhesive or glue.

Screwing Risers to Treads. Check the back of the tread; typically it's attached to the bottom of the riser. If you find that this joint squeaks, close any gaps with a couple of 1½-inch wood screws driven through the back of the riser into the edge of the tread. Drill a pilot hole and countersink hole before inserting the screw. Be careful that you don't run the drill bit or screw through the tread surface.

Checking the Wedges. If the stairs are constructed with housed stringers, they probably have (or should have) wood wedges between the stringer and each tread and riser. If wedges

have worked themselves loose, coat them with glue then reinsert them. If wedges are missing, cut new ones from hardwood, such as oak.

Wedge the back of the riser board first. Coat a wedge with glue and tap it into place lightly using a hammer. The wedge should be a little longer than necessary. After it is snug, cut the end flush with the bottom of the tread and riser. Then install a horizontal wedge. Wedge both ends of one step before moving to the next one.

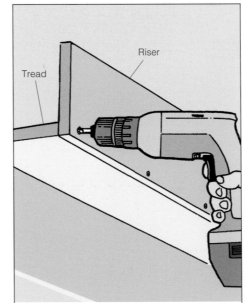

Shimming the Gaps. Squeaky treads may be owing to gaps between treads, risers, and skirtboard. Force wedges into these gaps using a little glue to hold them in place.

Replacing Angle Blocks. Angle blocks help prevent gaps from opening between risers and treads. Remove loose blocks; clean off old, dried glue; then reinstall the angle blocks.

Screwing Risers to Treads. Drive screws through the back of the riser into the tread to close a gap. Drill pilot holes for the screws to avoid splitting the riser.

Checking the Wedges. The wedges in housed stringers can work loose or even drop out. Reinsert loose wedges, or cut new ones if any are missing.

Eliminating Squeaks from Above

If you can't get underneath the stairs, you'll have to fix the squeaks from on top of the stairs.

Nailing the Front of the Tread. For squeaks at the front end of the tread, have a helper stand on the tread while you drive 8d finishing nails at opposing angles through the tread into the riser. Drill pilot holes first. Sink the heads of the nails with a nail set, and then fill the hole with putty.

Shimming the Tread. If you locate a squeak at the rear of the tread, drive glue-covered shims into the gap. Trim the shims with a utility knife, and use a damp rag to wipe off the excess glue. To cover the gap, install quarter-round or other decorative molding. Be sure that the molding won't reduce the tread depth below 9 inches.

This procedure will work just as well on gaps along the side of the treads or risers, where they abut a skirtboard.

Fastening the Tread. If you suspect that the squeak is due to a gap between the tread or riser and the stringer, you need to drive 2½-inch screws or 8d finishing nails through the tread into the stringer. The trick is locating the stringers. Usually, they're between ¾ inch and 2 inches from the edge of the tread, depending on whether or not the tread ends overhang the stringers. The third stringer should be in the center. Sink the nailheads with a nail set, then fill the holes with putty and sand the surface. To hide a screwhead, countersink the screw and fill the hole with a glued wood plug. For improved appearance, turn the plug's wood grain in the same direction as that of the tread.

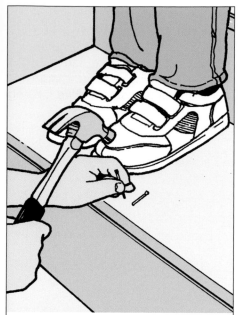

Nailing the Front of the Tread. Put weight on the front of the tread, and drive opposing 8d finishing nails.

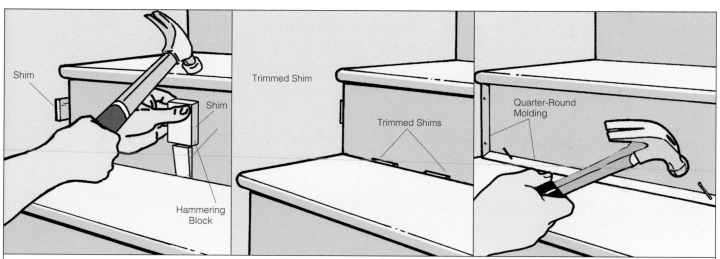

Shimming the Tread. Shim the rear of the tread; cut the shims flush with the riser; and attach decorative molding.

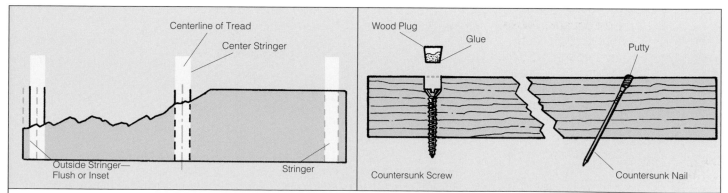

Fastening the Tread. Locate stringers at both ends and in the middle of the tread. Drive screws or nails into the treads, and cover them with wood plugs or putty, respectively.

Repairing Treads

Stair treads take a lot of abuse, so it's not unusual for one or more to need repair or replacement. Repair should be your first course of action. It's usually cheaper and quicker, and one new tread will look out of place among a stairway full of well-worn treads.

Removing a Tread. Usually, treads can be removed without disturbing risers. It is best to pry the tread off. Use a pry bar to remove any molding or nosing from the tread. Protect the riser with a thin piece of wood under the pry bar. Try to remove balusters from the tread without damaging them. If this is impossible, see "Replacing Balusters," page 74, for further advice. Finally, pry the tread loose enough to lift the nailheads, then remove the nails with the pry bar or a claw hammer.

Cutting Out a Tread. You may not be able to pry a tread out if it is fastened to the riser or if your stairs have housed stringers. In this case, you'll have to cut it out. Try to keep it as intact as possible, however, so that you can use it as a template to lay out a new tread.

To cut out a tread, drill a starter hole through the tread; then cut it using a keyhole saw or reciprocating saw. Carefully cut the front edge of the tread until you're able to pull it up and break it in half. Avoid cutting through the riser and stringers underneath. Use a chisel to remove any remaining wood. Then cut and install the new tread.

Repairing a Split Tread. If a tread is split, try to repair it before opting for a replacement. Remove the tread; then

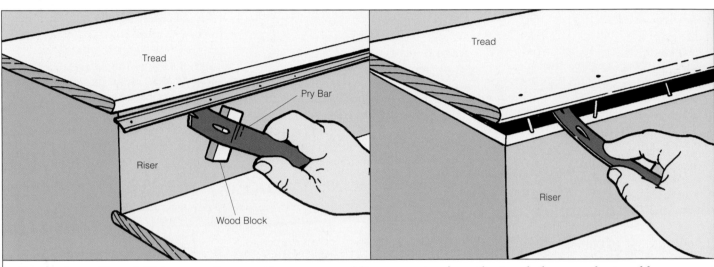

Removing a Tread. Using a pry bar, gently remove molding or nosing from the tread, then pry the tread loose enough to remove the nails. Put a piece of wood under the pry bar to protect risers and skirtboards from damage.

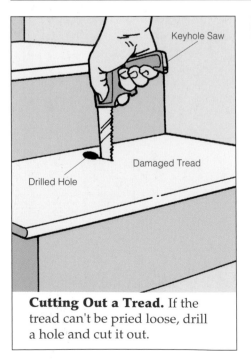

Cutting Out a Tread. If the tread can't be pried loose, drill a hole and cut it out.

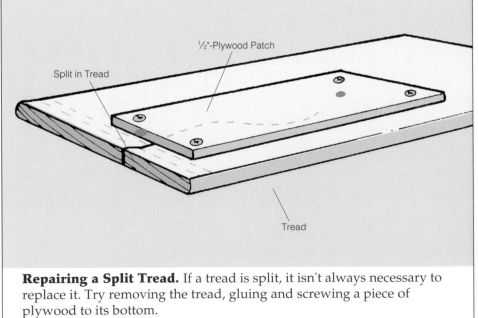

Repairing a Split Tread. If a tread is split, it isn't always necessary to replace it. Try removing the tread, gluing and screwing a piece of plywood to its bottom.

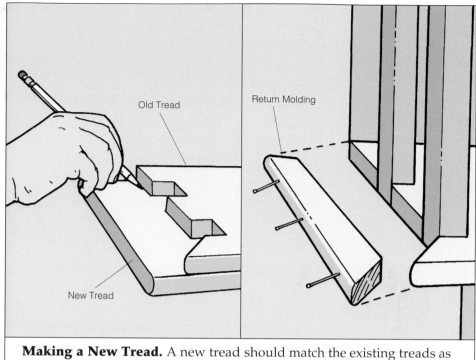

Making a New Tread. A new tread should match the existing treads as much as possible. Use the old tread to lay out the new one.

Tightening Loose Balusters

A baluster can loosen at the top or bottom. Often, balusters butt directly under the handrail and are toenailed in place. Sometimes, the butt joint isn't perfect, causing a gap between the baluster and the handrail. The baluster also can split from the nail and separate from the handrail.

Repairing the Handrail-Baluster Joint. If your problem is located at the handrail-baluster joint, first determine the extent of the damage. If the baluster is badly split from nailing or if there is a significant gap at the joint, you may need to replace the baluster. (For more information, see "Replacing Balusters," page 74.) If the baluster can be salvaged, you can remedy the problem with a wedge or a screw.

If the butt joint isn't tight, cut a thin wedge as wide as the baluster and slip the wedge into the joint where the gap is widest. Test the fit until you are satisfied; then spread glue on the wedge and tap it into the gap with a mallet. When the glue dries, use a chisel or utility knife to trim the wedge flush with the

cut a piece of plywood large enough to lap the split. Attach the plywood to the underside of the tread with glue and screws. This technique won't remove the split, of course, but it may stop any further damage.

Making a New Tread. To make a new tread, find a piece of wood that matches the other treads. Use the old tread as a template to lay out the new one. With a chisel or sandpaper, clean any glue from the edges of the old tread, balusters, and molding. Then trace the old tread's outline on the new wood. Cut out the new tread; then spread glue on all of the wood-to-wood joints. Set the tread in place, and secure it with screws or nails. Replace the balusters and molding.

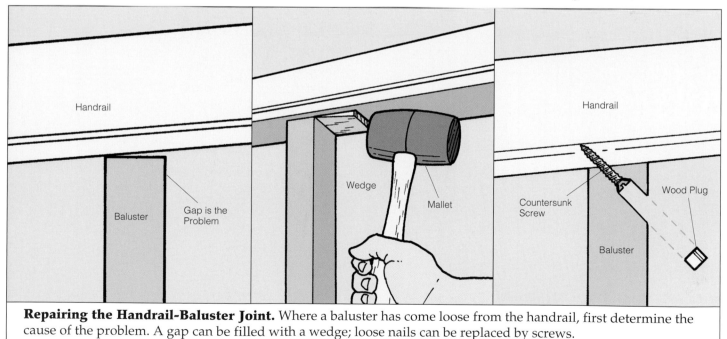

Repairing the Handrail-Baluster Joint. Where a baluster has come loose from the handrail, first determine the cause of the problem. A gap can be filled with a wedge; loose nails can be replaced by screws.

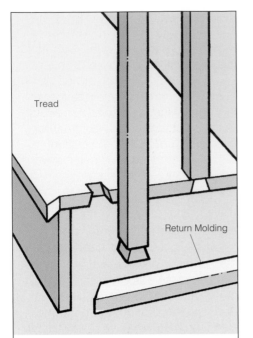

Repairing the Tread-Baluster Joint. A loose baluster may be due to a failed glue joint on the dovetail. Carefully remove the molding, and tap the baluster loose. Clean the mating surfaces, reglue, and reassemble.

baluster. Touch up the area with paint, if necessary.

If loose nails are the problem, try to remove them. Then drive a screw through the baluster into the handrail (drill a pilot hole first). If you are concerned about appearance, countersink the screw and cover it with a wood plug.

Repairing the Tread-Baluster Joint. At the bottom, balusters are typically attached to treads either with dowels or dovetails. If a doweled baluster is spinning in place, try to pry it up enough to inject some glue on the dowel. If this doesn't work, try toenailing the baluster. Or you may need to remove the baluster; clean the mating ends; then reglue and reinstall them. If you can't remove the baluster, you'll have to replace it. (See "Replacing Balusters," right.)

Usually, a dovetailed baluster is covered by a piece of return molding on the side of the tread. Carefully pry the molding off. If the dovetailed baluster is loose, tap it out with a

rubber hammer. Clean the old glue off all surfaces, then reinsert the freshly glued baluster in the tread. If you find a serious gap in the dovetail joint, fill it with a thin strip of wood.

Replacing Balusters

If you choose to replace a baluster, consider that you may have problems matching the new balusters to the old. You may be able to find a suitable replacement at your building-supply store. Ask to look through its catalogs if you can't find what you need. Or you can ask a woodturner to make a replacement. If several balusters need replacement, the best choice may be to tear them all out and replace them with a matched set.

Replacing a Doweled Baluster. If the ends of the tread overhang the stringers but there's no return molding on the tread ends, the balusters are probably fastened to the treads with pins or dowels. Saw through the baluster. If the joints are loose, you should be able to

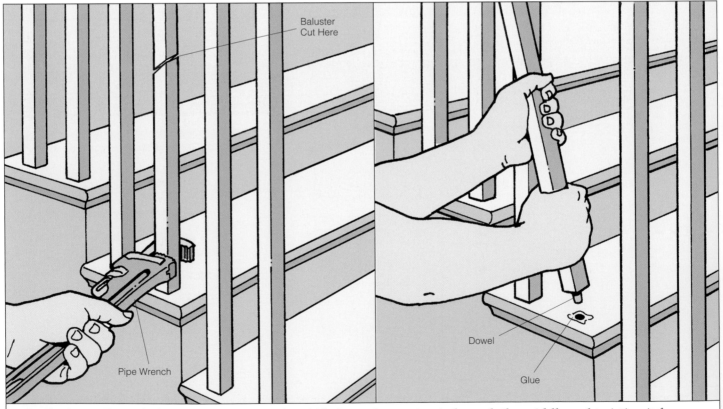

Replacing a Doweled Baluster. Remove the old baluster by sawing it through the middle and twisting it free with a pipe wrench. Thoroughly clean the hole in the tread before installing the new baluster.

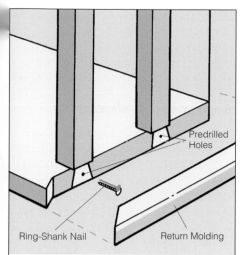

Ring-Shank Nail · Predrilled Holes · Return Molding

Replacing a Dovetailed Baluster. Remove the return molding, and tap the old baluster loose. When installing the replacement baluster, screw or nail it through the dovetail.

pull out both halves. If not, twist the baluster using a large adjustable wrench. You may be able to twist the baluster and dowel away from the tread. Clean the dried glue out of the hole in the tread, and cut the replacement baluster to length. Apply glue to both ends of the baluster and to the holes in the tread and handrail, then slip the top of the baluster in place. You will need to apply pressure to slip the bottom into place. Rotate the baluster into alignment before the glue sets.

If you can't remove the dowel from the tread, cut it off flush with the tread surface (being careful not to mar the surface), and bore out the dowel with a drill bit of equal diameter.

Replacing a Dovetailed Baluster.
Use a pry bar to remove the return

molding. Tap the dovetail loose by lightly hammering on the baluster, and then pry the baluster loose at the top (if it's nailed on) or remove the screw. Clean the tread and handrail of old glue. Cut the new baluster to length and install it. Glue the mating surfaces or, better yet, glue the joint and drive a nail or screw through a pilot hole in the dovetail into the tread. Replace the molding.

Replacing a Filleted Baluster.
If the baluster is encased at the bottom inside a skirtboard or at the top in a groove on the handrail, it may be held in place by fillets, or thin pieces of wood, which are often glued in place. Chisel out the fillet from under the handrail and at the skirtboard. You may need to remove the skirtboard first. Then remove the baluster. Cut the new baluster to length, make a new fillet or fillets. Toenail the baluster in place and glue the fillets beside it.

Newel Repairs

Because newel posts are located at the ends of the stairs, they're especially prone to loosening and damage. A loose newel can be dangerous and, if not repaired, can lead to more problems with the balustrade and railing. Tightening the newel can be quite complicated, depending on whether the newel is hollow or solid. If you can remove the cap, look inside the newel to see whether you have a hollow newel post. If you find the newel bolted to framing or if the newel post doesn't have a cap at all, it's solid.

Tightening a Hollow Newel

Usually, hollow newel posts are fastened by means of a threaded rod. The rod may run vertically from the top to the bottom of the newel, or it may be a horizontal connection between the newel and the bottom step on the staircase.

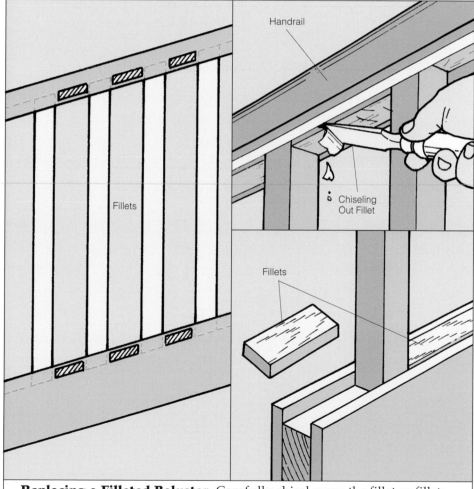

Handrail · Chiseling Out Fillet · Fillets · Fillets

Replacing a Filleted Baluster. Carefully chisel away the fillet or fillets holding the baluster in place. Replace the baluster and fillets, which fit inside a plowed handrail at the top and inside a skirtboard at the bottom.

To gain access to the top of a vertical threaded rod, remove the newel cap. The cap may be threaded on; if it's not threaded, you might have to tap it loose using a rubber mallet. With the cap removed, tighten the nut on the top end of the rod, either where you just removed the cap or immediately below where the cap fits. The bottom of the rod may be attached beneath the subflooring. If you can find the rod from the lower level and you can get access to it, tighten the nut on that end as well.

Often, the end of a lower horizontal rod can be located by removing a plug on the newel post and, if necessary, removing the bottom riser or tread. Wherever it's easiest to get access, tighten the nut on the newel or within the lower step to firm up a loose newel post

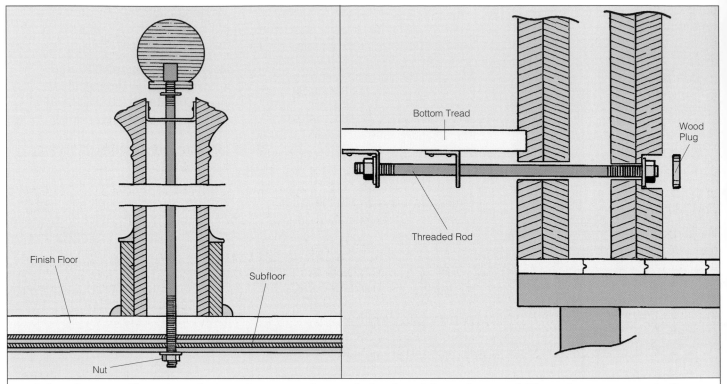

Tightening a Hollow Newel. Turn the nut on the treaded rod to tighten the newel. The rod may run vertically through the newel and under the subfloor or horizontally beneath the bottom tread.

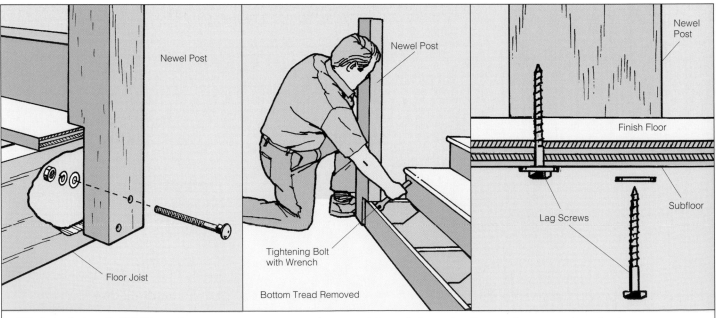

Tightening a Solid Newel. Try to gain access to the newel from below the floor or by removing the bottom tread. Tighten the fasteners, adding carriage bolts or lag screws if necessary.

Tightening a Solid Newel

A solid newel post may be bolted at the bottom to the stringer or to the joist beneath the floor. It could be connected with lag screws or carriage bolts and nuts. Depending on the construction, you can gain access either from a lower level or through the riser or tread at the bottom of the staircase. Tighten all of the fasteners you can reach.

If the newel post extends through the subfloor to the framing and you find only a single carriage bolt, drill a hole and add another bolt, washer, and nut. If the newel rests on the subfloor, drill additional holes from below into the bottom of the newel post, and secure the post with lag screws.

If you can't gain access from below, then bolt the stringer and newel post together. This task is best done if you can lift the tread and run the lag screws through the stringer and into the newel post. Attaching the newel post in this way means no fasteners will show, and you don't have to plug any holes. If you can't gain access to the newel post and stringer from above or below, you may be able to drill a pilot hole through the newel and into the stringer, then install a lag screw. Fill the resulting hole with a wood plug or dowel.

Tightening the Handrail

There are several ways in which a handrail can loosen, depending on how and where it is fastened. Handrails along the wall side of a staircase are usually attached to brackets that are screwed to the wall. Handrails on the open side of a staircase may be attached to a newel post at the bottom of the stairs and to the balusters along the handrail's length.

Securing a Wall Rail

The handrail brackets attached to the wall should be screwed through the wall into studs or blocking between the studs. If the bracket screws are loose, tighten them. If tightening doesn't work, install larger screws or reposition the handrail bracket so that you can drive the screws into new holes.

If none of these approaches work, the problem may be that the brackets aren't connected to a stud or blocking in the wall. It is doubtful that a decent carpenter would make such a mistake, but a previous homeowner may have unwittingly done so. Find the nearest stud with an electronic stud finder, by probing the wall with a scratch awl, or by lightly tapping on the wall with your knuckle; then reposition the brackets.

Securing a Balustrade Handrail

Usually, the handrail is attached to the newel post and the balusters, so the looseness you feel in the handrail may in fact be caused by a loose newel or balusters. First test the whole railing in an effort to determine the origin of the problem. If the newel post or balusters are loose, refer to the sections on repairing them, beginning on page 73.

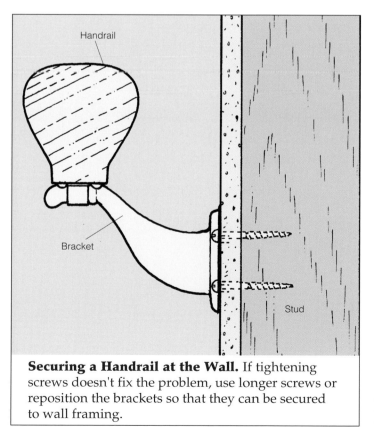

Securing a Handrail at the Wall. If tightening screws doesn't fix the problem, use longer screws or reposition the brackets so that they can be secured to wall framing.

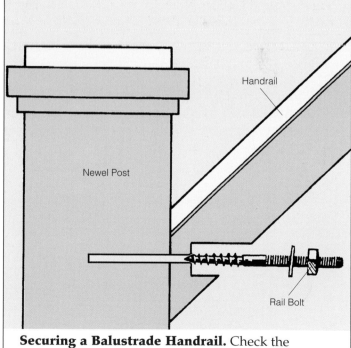

Securing a Balustrade Handrail. Check the newels, balusters, and handrail to determine the source of the problem. If the handrail is loose at the newel, tighten the star nut or rail-bolt nut.

Hollow Newels. A handrail may appear loose because of a poor connection at the newel post. First determine what type of newel you're dealing with: hollow or solid. Handrails are commonly attached to hollow newel posts with rail bolts and are held fast by means of a regular nut, which can be tightened using a socket wrench, or a star nut. A star nut is used when you can't get access to the nut with a wrench of any kind. It has slots into which you slip a screwdriver. You tap on the screwdriver with a hammer to tighten the nut. You can usually gain access to this assembly through the bottom side of the handrail. You may have to remove a wood plug first.

Solid Newels. With a solid newel post, the handrail is often attached with a counterbored rail bolt on the bottom. You may need a deep-throated socket wrench to tighten the nut on the rail bolt. If you find that the handrail is simply nailed to the newel post, remove the nails and install a rail bolt, as described in "Fastening Handrails to Newels," page 59.

Making Structural Repairs

If the stairs have several of the symptoms discussed above or if they are tilting or sagging, the problem may be of a structural nature. A failing staircase can be hazardous, so consider carefully whether you feel competent enough to make the correct diagnosis and proper repair.

Before you can investigate, you need to get under the staircase. If necessary, remove enough plaster and lath, drywall, or other wall covering to gain access to the underside of the staircase assembly. With the stairs exposed, begin your investigation. If the stairs sag on one side or the other, see whether the stringers have pulled away from the wall to which they were nailed or screwed. An old method of stairbuilding had one stringer attached only to the wall, without resting on any floor surface at all. All of the structural support came from the nails used to

fasten the stringer to the wall. You may be able to fix a sagging stair by securely nailing the stringer to the wall with 16d common nails.

Check to see whether the tops of the stringers have loosened from the header joist. Use metal angle brackets or joist hangers to resecure this connection.

If you find wood that has rotted or split badly, replace it. If the wood damage is more localized, you may be able to strengthen it by "sistering" another piece of lumber or plywood to it. The replacement wood must be large enough to connect with good, solid wood on all sides.

On older stairs with housed stringers, the middle stringer is often an un-notched 4x6 or 2x8 that was attached at the top and bottom to the inside of a header joist. If you find that such a stringer has pulled away from either header, reinforce the connection with heavy-duty (⅛- or ¼-inch-thick) angle iron attached with lag screws or carriage bolts. This kind of stringer can be improved substantially by adding plywood supports under each tread, alternating sides along the length of the stringer.

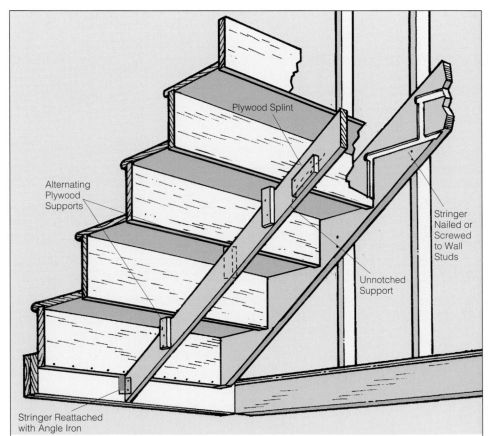

Making Structural Repairs. Loose stringers can be resecured to the wall framing with a few nails. A split in a stringer can be mended by "sistering" another piece of wood to it. Unnotched stringers may need to be reinforced at the header joist with heavy duty angle iron.

chapter 9

stone steps

Landscape Steps

Stone steps can add a distinctive look to your home landscape. In a sloping yard, a set of steps—even if it is just one or two—can make transitions easier when walking from one area to another. In many cases, the design and construction need not be as meticulous as stairs found indoors—although you must always make sure that the steps are safe to use. As you will see, you have your choice of dry-laid steps or fixing the stones in mortar. Build your steps from stone found in your yard or use exotic types that you purchase elsewhere.

Flagstone Steps

Flagstone is a traditional and proven material for patios and steps. It is sold in several thicknesses (generally from 1 to 2 inches) and in muted colors with subtle shadings that help your installation blend with the landscape. There are many ways to lay a flagstone patio and build steps. The most durable method is to pour a concrete slab and embed the stones in its surface. More often, flagstones are laid in sand on a bed of fine compacted gravel or a mixture of compacted dirt and sand. Sand is useful for screeding to a pitch of about one percent for drainage. Using random shapes is the most challenging approach and creates the greatest waste. You can also use square-cut flagstones designed to fit together in several modular patterns that reduce cutting time.

Flagstone Patio & Steps

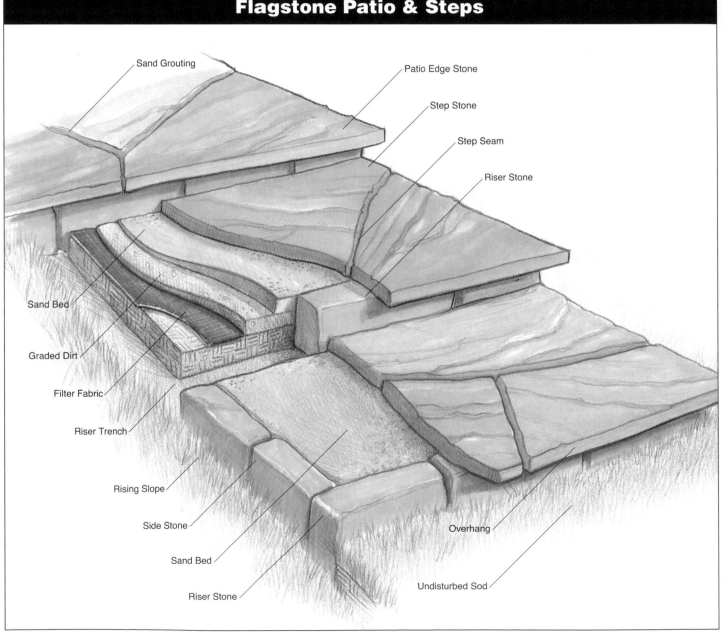

Sand Grouting · Patio Edge Stone · Step Stone · Step Seam · Riser Stone · Sand Bed · Graded Dirt · Filter Fabric · Riser Trench · Rising Slope · Side Stone · Sand Bed · Riser Stone · Overhang · Undisturbed Sod

Flagstone Patio & Steps Installation

Tools
- Work gloves
- Shovel and tamper
- Spirit level and measuring tape
- Clamps ■ Mortar mixing box
- Mixing hoe ■ Hammer
- Rubber mallet and cold chisel
- Push broom
- Garden hose with spray head

Materials
- Stone
- Gravel base
- Filter fabric
- Screeding sand
- Mortar mix
- Stakes
- Layout string

Smart Job Tip
To increase the durability of grouted seams between stones you can add cement to the sand before brushing it into cracks. Using only sand, you'll have to come back after a day or two to refill the joints that settle after wetting. Another approach is to leave larger gaps, fill with topsoil, and sow grass seed in the seams.

1 Use stakes and strings to lay out the patio and steps. Remove the sod from the area.

2 Dig a shallow trench to embed the edging support stones below the graded patio level.

3 Use a hand tamper or the end of a 2x4 to compact the dirt in the trench.

4 Set the edge stones in the trench so that the tops will be level with the screeded sand of the patio.

Planning Layout Patterns

The most reliable way to establish the sizes of treads and risers is to stake a long, straight, and level board along the edge of the slope. This allows you to try several combinations. For example, you can extend the treads 18 inches or more to reach a comfortable maximum of 6- or 7-inch risers, or reduce them to achieve a comfortable minimum of about 4-inch risers.

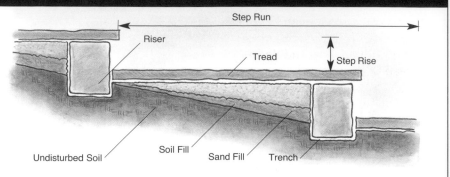

5 Spreading a layer of filter fabric or black plastic can suppress weed growth through patio joints.

6 Cover the excavation with at least 2 in. of sand, and use a straight board to screed the surface.

9 Set up a level board to gauge the slope, and lay out the treads and risers of the steps.

10 Measure down from the level board at the edge of the tread to establish the step rise.

The key to working with heavy stones is leverage. You'll want to move stones with pry bars and dollies instead of with your back, arms, and legs. For clearing and moving large rocks of any kind, consider investing in an oversize pry bar, generally called a wrecking bar. A dolly is very handy, considering that a delivered pallet of flagstones weighs about 3,000 pounds.

Wrecking bars are long pry bars that apply exceptional leverage.

A dolly is handy for transporting stones around the worksite.

7 Set the perimeter flagstones in the screeded sand, laying the straightest edges to the outside.

8 Embed flagstones using a rubber mallet. Check the surface with a straightedge and/or level.

11 Set up stakes and strings to mark the treads and guide excavation work on the slope.

12 Dig a shallow trench at the outer edge of each tread so that you can embed riser stones.

9 Stone Steps

A typical delivery of rough flagstones contains many shapes and sizes that are graded by color and width. You can also order cut stones that fit together neatly. With rough material you need to carefully plan the intricate joints on patios and steps. Narrow, sand-filled seams generally require some trimming, while wider seams make greater use of existing shapes.

Consistently narrow joints filled with sand require a puzzle-like fit.

Wider, grass-filled joints are easier to plan and create less waste.

13 Set and level the riser stones for the steps. You'll need to remove the sod before screeding.

14 Compact the area behind the risers, add sand, screed the bed, and check for level.

17 Embed flagstones in the sand to form the steps. It's wise to work out the patterns in advance.

18 You can grout the flagstone joints with sand or a mix of 4 parts sand and 1 part dry mortar.

Even within the standard size categories of 1- and 2-inch flagstone, it's common to find variations of ¼ inch either way. That means one step stone could be up to ½ inch thicker than the next one. Compensate by shimming with flakes of stone. To keep a shim from shifting and the step from sinking, embed the shim in a small mound of mortar.

Check for level, and measure the thickness of the required shim.

Keep the shim stone from shifting by embedding it in mortar.

15 Follow the same procedures as you work down the slope, maintaining the tread and riser sizes.

16 Check the riser stones by leveling from step to step with scraps of flagstone in place.

19 Push the sand mix back and forth across the patio and steps with a broom, filling the joints.

20 Spray the sand with water, and refill and respray the joints after the first layer settles.

Step Design

Some people add steps to their landscape not out of necessity, but because they like the way they look. If your slope is less than 10 percent, meaning that, it rises less than 1 foot in 10 feet of run, then steps are optional. However, one or more single steps can add texture and interest along a gently sloping path.

All types of steps have a few design considerations in common.

Rise and Run

The surface of the steps on which you walk is called the tread. The height or distance from the top of one tread to the top of the next is called the unit rise. It is the relationship between the depth of the tread (unit run) and the height of the unit rise that determines how comfortable the steps are to use. Typically, the taller the unit rise, the shallower the tread. As a rule of thumb for exterior steps, the combined length of one tread and two risers should be 25 to 27 inches.

Similarly, a recommended range for the rise between any two steps is 5 to 7 inches. This gives you a tread depth of between 15 and 17 inches. Many landscape designers favor a 15-inch run and 6-inch rise for garden steps.

Finding the Rise and Run. Before you can make a decision about the unit rise and run, you need to calculate the total rise and run for the stairs. Rise refers to the vertical distance from the bottom of the first step to the top of the top step. Run refers to the horizontal distance from the front of the lowest step to the back of the top step.

To calculate these distances, drive a short stake at the point at which you want the top of the steps to start, and use a tall stake to indicate the front edge of the bottom step. Attach a string at ground level to the bottom of the short stake; stretch it taut; and tie it to the tall stake. Use a line level to level the string. Measure the distance from the string to the ground at the tall stake: this distance equals the total rise—the combined height of each step. To find the run, measure the distance between the stakes. (See "Step Layout," below.)

Deep treads are common in landscape steps, above. They encourage people to stop and enjoy the view.

Step Layout

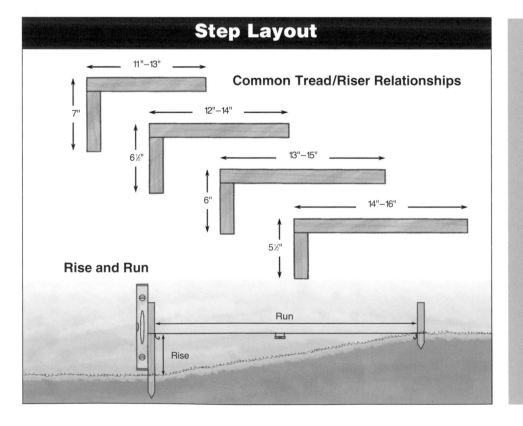

Common Tread/Riser Relationships

11"–13" 7"

12"–14" 6½"

13"–15" 6"

14"–16" 5½"

Rise and Run

Run

Rise

Altering the Run

Here are ways to alter the run of your steps.

■ At the bottom or top of the stairs, slope and landscape the adjacent grade to fit a more comfortable unit run/unit rise ratio in the space you have.

■ Add a landing part way up the steps.

■ Add bends or curves to the steps to lengthen the run.

■ Build a stone landing at the bottom of the steps that has a rise that is different from the rise of the first step.

■ Make the top tread deeper.

These stairs make it easy to reach the plants on the hillside, top right.

Stairs made of dressed stone, bottom right, add a touch of formality to this garden.

Each of these steps is actually a large landing, which is acceptable for landscape steps, below.

Calculate Unit Rise and Run

Once you know the total rise and run, you can figure out the unit rise and run. To determine the unit rise, divide the total rise by the potential number of steps. If your answer is less or more than 5 to 7 inches, you may want to adjust the number of steps. For example, if the total rise is 38 inches and you have five steps in mind, you'd have a riser height of 7.6 inches. But six steps will give you a unit rise of 6.3 inches (38 ÷ 6 = 6.3), well within the ideal range for outdoor steps.

Tread Depth. Now use your unit rise dimension to calculate the tread depth, or unit run. Using the measurements 1 tread + 2 risers = 25 to 27 inches as a guide, in our example, twice the unit rise is 12.6. If you subtract that from 25 and 27 you end up with treads somewhere between 12.4 and 14.4 inches deep.

Now multiply the depth of the treads by the number of steps. Does it equal the total run? Most likely it will not. When your initial rise and run combination doesn't fit into the ideal range, make adjustments to design steps that are safe and comfortable to use. As a safety precaution, maintain the same riser height for all the steps in a flight. For tips on making adjustments, see "Altering the Run," on page 86.

Step Width

In addition to aesthetic consider-ations, think about how you will use the steps. If they are in a garden where you often walk with another person, you may want steps at least 5 feet wide. Four feet is a generous width for one person. In a less formal garden, stone steps as narrow as 16 inches may be adequate. The layout and construct-ion is basically the same regardless of the size of the stones you use.

The way the steps fit in with the scale of the surroundings is another important consideration in choosing

a step width. For example, steps from a large patio would be wider than steps adjacent to a smaller patio. Steps leading away from high traffic areas are generally smaller than those used as a main entrance.

"Steps through a Wall," above, shows how to make wide steps without having to handle massive individual stones. Many people prefer steps constructed from large stones because of their dramatic design qualities. If you have your heart set on steps made from individual large stones, you will need equipment and an operator to move them into place. If you want to set the stones yourself, you may be able to rent a small bobcat locally. You can also set moderately large stones with a 40-horsepower or larger tractor and bucket.

Building Steps

After you decide on the size and number of steps, cut and fill the area where the steps will go. The process is similar to cutting and filling for terraced walls. As with most stone projects, the quality of the soil where the stone rests is just as important as the stone itself. Undisturbed, well-drained soils are best for building steps. In all other soils, excavate an additional 4 to 12 inches and backfill with gravel that packs and drains.

Ground covers allowed to spread along the riser, above, add an interesting design touch.

These steps, opposite top, may not be necessary, but they add texture and interest to the area.

This unusual combination, opposite bottom, teams individual stone risers with gravel treads.

Steps Through a Wall

Laying up steps as you would short sections of retainer wall is one way to build wide steps without having to use large stones and excavation equipment. This style of step is commonly used to make steps through a wall. The top tread can be made out of one or more stones. Using dressed stone for the tread gives a more formal appearance, but the uniform surface is a desirable feature, especially in high-traffic areas.

The First Step. There are three ways to set step stones: over-lapped, butted, and spaced. (See page 92.)

Beginning at the bottom of the flight, make sure that the first step is set securely. A good first step provides a firm foundation for the second step and so forth. Follow these guidelines.

■ The front edge of the first tread may rest on the hard surface of a patio or walkway.

■ Excavate and set a base stone that is level with or slightly above the adjacent grade.

- Remove the topsoil; replace it with gravel, sand, or stone; then set your first step on it. Add 4 to 6 inches of gravel—more if you are building on slow-draining soil.

- Create a landing area with a different rise than the rise between steps.

Set the Remaining Steps. Once the first step is set, continue setting the steps, using a mallet to firmly bed each stone. Check your work to maintain the same rise between the steps.

Inspect the steps after a hard rain, and make adjustments if a step rocks when you step on it. In climates with freezing temperatures, inspect steps each spring for dislodged stones.

Mortared Steps

Steps made with mortared flagging or pavers require a concrete foundation. However, before you can install the foundation, you must know the thickness of the stone in order to calculate the rise and run of the foundation. Add 1 to 1½ inches for mortar to your calculations.

If you use pavers, adjust your dimensions to use full-size pavers. If you use random-sized flagging, test-fit the stones before mixing the mortar.

Using Undressed Stone

If you use fieldstone or undressed quarry stone for landscape steps, adjust the depth of your excavation so that the rise between the steps remains constant.

Place large individual stones on a firm base; add well-draining gravel if necessary, opposite top.

Adding landings to your steps, opposite bottom, makes the climb more comfortable, and they provide a way to adjust the rise-and-tread relationship.

Narrow garden steps complement this informal hillside rock garden, above.

Consider combining materials for steps. Here landscape ties and gravel work together to form steps, right.

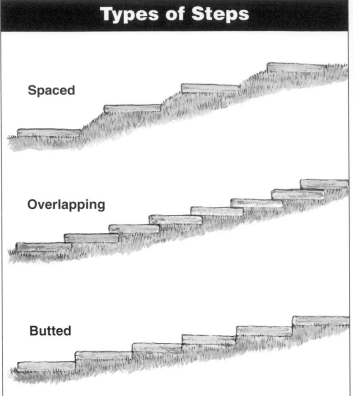

Types of Steps

Spaced

Overlapping

Butted

If you are using large treads of dressed stone, above, adjust the width of the stairs to eliminate cutting.

Spend time setting the first step; it will provide the foundation for the next steps, below.

Short walls in a terraced yard provide ready-made steps. Add plants to the terraces for impact, below right.

Mortared steps, opposite right, require a concrete base. Include the thickness of the mortar bed in rise/run calculations.

Interior Fill Stones

Compacted Soil

Irregular Inner Face

Square Outer Face

Tread Cap Stone

Covered Joint

4"–6" Gravel

Footing Stone

Inspect steps each spring for damage that may have occurred over the winter, left. Look for loose stones.

Steps, patios, and walls made from the same type of stone create a unified design, above.

This unique design consists of wood dividers that separate blue small-dimension stone, below.

glossary

Glossary/Index

Angle Blocks Triangular blocks of wood attached with adhesive and nails to the underside of the stairs at the junction where the tread meets the riser.

Balusters Small vertical members that usually support the handrail.

Balustrade The entire assembly that supports the handrail. It consists of newels, balusters, and the handrail.

Bracketed Stringer An unnotched stringer that has a special metal bracket attached to the inside to support treads.

Cleated Stringer An unnotched stringer that has wood cleats screwed to the inside to carry treads.

Closed Riser A kind of staircase with risers installed between treads.

Dadoed Stringer A mortised stringer with channels cut on the inside faces to hold the treads.

Dovetailed Baluster Balusters that are attached to treads with dovetail joints. An old-fashioned method of construction.

Filleted Balustrade A balustrade consisting of spaces filled with short pieces of wood between balusters.

Finial An ornamental projection (on a newel, for example).

Folding Attic Stairs Stairs easily pulled down to provide access.

Gooseneck The uppermost section of a curved staircase fitting.

Handrail The part of the balustrade (and wall rail) that is grasped.

Hangerboard On interior stairs, the piece of ¾-inch plywood that is nailed to the upper framing.

Headroom The vertical distance from the nosing to any object above.

Hollow Newel A newel post attached to the subfloor with a threaded rod.

Housed Stringer A form of staircase construction in which the stringer has tapered mortises routed into the face of the finish stringer. Treads and risers slip into the mortises and are secured with wedges.

Kickboard The 2x4 wood member at the base of the stairs that is notched into the stringers.

Ladder Any stairway in which the slope exceeds acceptable rise and run requirements.

Landing A horizontal platform at mid-flight in a staircase. Most often necessary on stairs that change directions.

L-Shaped Stairs A stairway that makes a 90-degree turn.

Mortised Stringer A stringer in which recesses have been cut to accept treads and sometimes risers.

Newel A large vertical member to which the handrail is attached. Newels provide structural support for the balustrade.

Nosing That part of the tread that overhangs the face of the riser. Nosings are often rounded.

Notched Stringer A stringer that has been cut out in a sawtooth pattern to support treads and risers.

Open Riser A staircase in which the vertical space between treads is left open.

Over-the-Post Railing A balustrade in which a continuous handrail is attached to the tops of the newel posts.

Pinned Baluster Manufactured balusters with wood pins on the base that fit into holes bored in the treads.

Pitch Block A triangular piece of wood with sides equal to the rise, run, and slope of the stairs. Used as a guide for a drill when building the underside of a handrail.

Platform Stairs Stairs built for access to a low deck or patio without the hassle of stringers.

Post-to-Post Railing A balustrade in which the handrail is cut to fit between newel posts.

Rabbet A ledge cut along one edge of a workpiece.

Rise A vertical measurement of stairway height.

Riser The vertical part of the stair, located between treads.

Round-Top Baluster Any baluster with rounded ends for fitting.

Run A horizontal measurement of stairway length.

Skirtboard A piece of trim installed between the stairs and a wall.

Solid Newel A newel post bolted to the house frame.

Spiral Stairs Stairs that rise in a spiral, usually made from premanufactured kits. Spiral stairs provide limited access and should never be used as primary stairs.

Stair Bracket A metal support fastened to the wall that is attached to the handrail.

Stairwell The framed hole in the floor through which stairs pass.

Straight-Run Stairs A staircase that rises in a straight line from bottom to top.

Stringers The structural support members to which treads are attached. Also called carriage.

Total Rise The total vertical distance through which the stairs must cross, from finished floor to finished floor.

Total Run The total horizontal distance the stairs cover from the face of the top riser to that of the bottom riser.

Tread The horizontal part of the stair on which one steps. The nosing is technically part of the tread.

Unit Rise The vertical distance from one tread to the next.

Unit Run The horizontal distance from the face of one riser to that of the next.

U-shaped Stairs Also called switchback stairs, they make a 180-degree turn.

Utility Staircase A less frequently used staircase, usually built for access to an attic or basement.

Wall Rail The handrail attached to the wall in an enclosed stairwell.

Winder An L-shaped staircase that uses wedge-shaped treads to make a sweeping 90-degree turn.

index